LIQUID CITY

Megalopolis and the Contemporary Northeast

John Rennie Short

Resources for the Future
Washington, DC, USA

An RFF Press book
Published by Resources for the Future
1616 P Street NW
Washington, DC 20036–1400
USA
www.rffpress.org

Library of Congress Cataloging-in-Publication Data

Short, John R.
  Liquid city : megalopolis and the contemporary northeast / John Rennie Short.
    p. cm.
  Includes bibliographical references and index.
  ISBN 978-1-933115-49-8 (hardcover : alk. paper) -- ISBN
978-1-933115-50-4 (pbk. : alk. paper) 1. Metropolitan areas--Middle
Atlantic States. 2. Sociology, Urban--Middle Atlantic States. 3.
Middle Atlantic States--Population. 4. Middle Atlantic States--Economic
conditions--21st century. I. Title.
  HT334.M53S46 2007
  307.76'40974--dc22

                                                    2007011499

The paper in this book meets the guidelines for permanence and durability of the Committee on Production Guidelines for Book Longevity of the Council on Library Resources. This book was typeset by Jeff Hall. It was copyedited by Sally Atwater. The cover was designed by Henry Rosenbohm.

ISBN 978-1-933115-49-8 (cloth)   ISBN 978-1-933115-50-4 (paper)

About Resources for the Future *and* RFF Press

Resources for the Future (RFF) improves environmental and natural resource policymaking worldwide through independent social science research of the highest caliber. Founded in 1952, RFF pioneered the application of economics as a tool for developing more effective policy about the use and conservation of natural resources. Its scholars continue to employ social science methods to analyze critical issues concerning pollution control, energy policy, land and water use, hazardous waste, climate change, biodiversity, and the environmental challenges of developing countries.

RFF Press supports the mission of RFF by publishing book-length works that present a broad range of approaches to the study of natural resources and the environment. Its authors and editors include RFF staff, researchers from the larger academic and policy communities, and journalists. Audiences for publications by RFF Press include all of the participants in the policymaking process—scholars, the media, advocacy groups, NGOs, professionals in business and government, and the public.

CONTENTS

FIGURES AND TABLES

FIGURES

TABLES

ACKNOWLEDGMENTS

Books may have individual authors but they always embody collaborations. A number of people assisted in the production of this book. Nadwa Mossaad was my graduate research assistant for a year at an early stage of the project and collected many of the data. Michael Sturtevant created the geographic information system that helped me analyze these data and, with fellow undergraduate student Patrick Hipp, helped in the creation of some of the maps. At the final stage of the project, another undergraduate student, Brendan Bartow, also helped with the maps.

Tom Rabenhorst and his students provided the maps for the electronic atlas of Megalopolis. The atlas is available at http://www.umbc.edu/ges/student_projects/digital_atlas/instructions.htm. My collaboration with Tom and his students aided my understanding of the spatial dynamics of Megalopolis.

Tom Frederickson, Mathew Kachura, and Keith Wiley wrote a number of data analysis papers in a graduate research class that widened my understanding of Megalopolis.

Invitations to speak to various audiences at the Institute of Civic Engagement at the State University of New York in Cortland, Johns Hopkins

University in Baltimore, the University of Amsterdam in the Netherlands, and the University of New South Wales in Sydney, Australia, forced me to formulate some of the arguments into a more coherent structure.

For the past three years Bernadette Hanlon and Tom Vicino have been my indispensable collaborators in a number of research projects. Many of the ideas and findings in this book emerged from their hard work.

Three anonymous reviewers made many good suggestions and identified some loose ends and frayed edges in the fabric of the argument. I thank them for their time and care.

For ideas to become books, there needs to be some encouragement. Don Reisman's quick and positive response and sound editorial suggestions provided that much-needed encouragement. Sally Atwater improved the text immeasurably with an excellent job of copyediting.

CHAPTER ONE

REVISITING MEGALOPOLIS

T he topic of this book is one of the world's most important metropolitan regions—Megalopolis, an area spanning 600 miles from
north of Richmond in Virginia to just north of Portland in Maine and from
the shores of the northern Atlantic to the Appalachians. Interstate 95 is its
spine, with major vertebrae at Washington, Baltimore, Philadelphia, New
York, and Boston. As one vast conurbation that covers 52,000 square miles
and contains 49 million people, Megalopolis is the densest urban agglomeration in the United States, one of the largest city regions on earth, an important element in the national economy, and a vital hub in a globalizing
world.

The term *megalopolis* has an interesting history: it was the name given
to a city in Peloponnese founded by Epaminondas around 371–368 BCE.
Megalopolis was planned on the grand scale: the city walls formed a circle
five miles in circumference. Great things were expected of the city, but it
failed to realize the dreams of the founders, and it declined by the late
Roman period. The term reemerged in the 20th century. The Scottish poly-
math and urban scholar and planner Patrick Geddes (1854–1932) first employed the term in 1927 to designate one of the latter stages in his model

1

of urban decline ranging from Metropolis to Necropolis. Geddes's disciple, the American Lewis Mumford (1895–1990) used the term and further developed the evolutionary model in his 1939 book, *The Culture of Cities*. For both Geddes and Mumford, *megalopolis* characterizes a degenerative stage of urban development in an era of giant cities, after the vitality of *metropolis* and before the exploitative *tyrannopolis* and the finality of *necropolis*, the city of war, famine, and abandonment.

Jean Gottmann (1915–1994) used *megalopolis* in 1957 to describe the urbanized Northeast of the United States. Gottmann's concept of megalopolis was much more optimistic and upbeat than the pessimistic model of Geddes and Mumford (Baigent 2004). It was a place of vitality and a harbinger of a better future, not a later stage in a trajectory of inexorable decline.

Gottmann's study drew upon data from the 1950 census. It is now time, indeed long past time, to take stock of this, the nation's largest urban region, and note and explain what has happened since 1950, in terms of both its internal changes and its wider role in the life of the nation. This book also assesses critically the main changes and evaluates which account was right about the trajectory of Megalopolis, the pessimistic account offered by Geddes and Mumford or the optimistic reading of Gottmann.

The book focuses on five main aspects of change in the region:

- population redistribution;
- economic restructuring;
- immigration;
- patterns of racial and ethnic segregation; and
- processes of globalization.

Chapter 2 discusses Gottmann's work and provides the basis for a more rigorous definition of Megalopolis. I make a case for the conceptual fluidity of today's Megalopolis. Chapter 3 considers the major trends in population redistribution. These include the relative decline of the region's share of national population, the marked suburbanization, the decline of central city areas apart from New York City, and the marked increase in the southern tier of the region, which includes the suburbs in Maryland and Virginia that encircle Washington, D.C. The reasons for and consequences of these changes will be discussed.

Chapter 4 measures and maps the level of deindustrialization, the growth of services, and the continuing vitality of advanced producer services and government employment. The consequences of these changes on different places and different groups of workers are noted.

Since the 1970s the level of immigration to the United States and this region has increased markedly. Areas of high immigration are noted in Chapter 5. Using data at a variety of scales and a mix of techniques (including the index of dissimilarity, the index of segregation, and the location quotient), Chapter 6 identifies patterns of segregation by race. I show that racial segregation remains an important feature of this region despite the enormous social changes.

There is now a greater awareness of the importance of scale in our understanding of social processes. Chapters 7, 8, and 9 look at the differences within Megalopolis at the scale of counties, census places, and census tracts, respectively. In Chapter 8, for example, analysis of census data allows the identification of five neighborhood types: middle America, affluent suburbs, underclass, black middle class, and immigrant gateways. Chapter 9 drops down to the finer-grained census tract level to identify the polarized city, the affluent city, the poor city, and areas of pronounced change.

In Chapter 10 I explore how this region embodies and reflects economic, political, and cultural globalization by drawing upon recent work that has developed ideas of large city regions as arenas of globalization. Chapter 11 addresses the regional issues that cut across the municipal and state boundaries within Megalopolis. Chapter 12 provides a summary of the main conclusions of the study.

I wrote this book for three reasons. First, when I moved to the Baltimore-Washington area in 2002, I remembered reading Gottmann's *Megalopolis* as a student and realized I was now living in this urban region. Situated between Baltimore and Washington, frequently traveling along I-95 and regularly taking the Acela Express train to New York, I was acutely aware of the spatial spread of the region. Studying where I live has been a feature of my research going back to my graduate student days at the University of Bristol, when I studied the dynamics of the local housing market (Short 1978). It continued when I moved closer to London and studied the M4 growth corridor that stretched from London to Reading (Short et al. 1986). Later, when I moved to the United States, I examined the renewal and reimagining of Syracuse as it tried to move beyond its rustbelt past and industrial image (Short et al. 1993). To move to Megalopolis was another opportunity for a locally based study, this time of a large urban region.

Second, because of the importance of Gottmann's work, I wanted to write an update prompted by the simplest of questions: what has happened in the region since his book was published? We have so few good baseline studies in the social sciences that it was a rare chance to do a follow-up study to ascertain elements of change as well as dimensions of stability.

Third, a study of the region provided an opportunity to do a case study of an emerging urban phenomenon. A number of recent studies are suggesting that large urban regions are the new building block of both national and global economies. Scholars have identified globalizing city regions in which most urban and industrial growth is concentrated (Scott 2001; Short 2004). Peter Taylor (2004) describes the world economy as structured around an archipelago of global city regions. In the developed world these city regions are the loci of control-and-command functions with a heavy concentration of advanced producer services, such as banking, advertising, and business services. In the developing world these are the site of multinational corporation investment and new techniques of manufacturing as well as centers of service industries. Three giant urban regions now exist in Asia Pacific—Bangkok (population 11 million), Seoul (20 million), and Jakarta (20 million), which attract 25 to 35 percent of all foreign direct investment into their respective countries and constitute 20 to 40 percent of the gross domestic product. In China, the three city regions of Beijing, Shanghai, and Hong Kong constitute less than 8 percent of the national population, yet they attract 73 percent of the foreign investment and produce 73 percent of all exports. China is less a national economy than three large urban economies.

Recent work that has looked at U.S. city regions, in part following on from Gottmann, has identified 10 megalopolitan regions, defined as clustered networks of metropolitan regions that either have populations of more than 10 million or will exceed that number, according to current growth projections, by 2040 (Lang and Dhavale 2005a; Table 1-1). Collectively, these large city regions constitute only 19.8 percent of the nation's land surface yet account for 67.4 percent of the population and approximately three-quarters of all predicted growth in population and construction from 2010 to 2040. The northeastern and mid-Atlantic area identified in this study, Megalopolis, is the largest of these regions in the country, responsible for 20 percent of the U.S. gross domestic product. Such connected metropolitan areas are increasingly recognized as the centers of economic gravity in both the country and the world. Although these regions have been identified in general outline, they have not been considered in great detail. Undertaking a case study of one of the larger and more important megaurban regions in the world allows an examination of a major building block of the globalizing economy.

Table 1-1.   Megalopolitan Regions in the United States

	Largest city	2000 population (millions)
Northeast and mid-Atlantic (Megalopolis)	New York	49.18
Midwest	Chicago	39.48
Southland	Los Angeles	20.96
Piedmont	Atlanta	18.39
I-35 Corridor	Dallas	14.46
Peninsula	Miami	12.83
Northern California	San Francisco	11.56
Gulf Coast	Houston	11.53
Cascadia	Seattle	7.11
Valley of the Sun	Phoenix	4.09

Source: Lang and Dhavale (2005a).

This book is also the final part in a trilogy of urban works. In *Urban Theory* (2006) I assessed the theoretical advances made in our understanding of the city, and in *Alabaster Cities* (2006) I applied them to an understanding of urban America since 1950. *Liquid City* follows up on the theoretical debates in *Urban Theory* and the historical context of *Alabaster Cities*.

The book thus constitutes a personal quest, a backward glance at a classic study, and an assessment of an urban form that is beginning to dominate both the national and the global economies. This study of Megalopolis represents a Janus-like sweep, considering both what has happened to one of the world's largest and most important urban regions and the likely course of future developments.

CHAPTER TWO

LIQUID CITY

Jean Gottmann applied the term *Megalopolis* to the urbanized Northeast of the United States. He described it as "an almost continuous stretch of urban and suburban areas from southern New Hampshire to northern Virginia and from the Atlantic shore to the Appalachian foothills" with a total population of 37 million people in 1960 (Gottmann 1961, 3). He first used the term in English in 1957 in an article published in *Economic Geographer,* where he prefigured the main arguments that would appear later in his better-known book, *Megalopolis* (Gottmann 1961).

The map that Gottmann used in the 1957 paper to delineate Megalopolis was drawn from an even earlier study, an innovative government survey to identify economic areas in the country (Bogue 1951). Using data from 1940, since the 1950 census data had not yet been released, the study looked at 164 variables (76 agricultural and 88 nonagricultural) for 3,101 counties in the United States. A total of 501 state economic areas were identified. The study noted a special class of area, termed *metropolitan state economic areas,* where "the nonagricultural economy … is a closely integrated unit and is distinctly different from the economy of the areas which lie outside the orbit or close contact with the metropolis" (Bogue 1951, 2). A total of 149 metropolitan state economic areas were found across the country. A national map of these economic areas depicted an area of metropolitan economy from Boston to Washington. Gottmann could see the important implications of this map. His genius lay in developing this observation into a wider debate and a deeper analysis.

Gottmann developed his ideas while he was working along the main corridor of Megalopolis. He had a thoroughly international outlook. His parents had been killed in the Russian Revolution. He moved to France, completed his doctorate at the University of Paris, and later fled to England in the wake of the Nazi persecution of Jews. He arrived as a refugee to the United States in 1942 and taught at Johns Hopkins University in Baltimore. He returned briefly to France after the war to teach at the Ecole des Hautes Etudes at the Sorbonne. He soon returned to the United States, where for the next 20 years he commuted between Boston, New York, Princeton, Baltimore, and Washington until he was appointed Professor of Geography at Oxford University in 1968. He began to work on the topic of *Megalopolis* in 1956 at the prompting of Robert Oppenheimer, then head of the Institute of Advanced Studies at Princeton. From 1956 to 1960 the Twentieth Century Fund underwrote his research.

In the 1961 book Gottmann describes the region as the "hinge of the American economy," containing a concentration of economic and cultural activities, a large number of academic and research institutions, a powerful political center in Washington, and a good transportation system that fosters economic connectivity. The book depicts a deeply interwoven urban-suburban area with dense population, supremacy in political and cultural activities, and concentrated economic activity and wealth. The book contains enormous detail, with lots of data, tables, and figures. It is an encyclopedic regional geography in the classic French tradition in which Gottmann had been schooled. But his book is also the recognition and celebration of a new order in the organization of inhabited space, in essence a new way of life. Gottmann saw the region as an incubator of new urbanization, a laboratory for a new experiment in social living. Like many immigrants to the United States from war-ravaged Europe, Gottmann reveled in the possibility of a society dedicated to the premise of a better tomorrow. He imbibed the New World optimism.

In a careful reading of Gottmann's work, Robert Lake (2003) draws attention to the assumptions behind the analysis: the celebration of size and growth, the sense of inevitability, a belief in unbounded entrepreneurialism, and consumer choice with a utopian emphasis on suburban dynamism. Little consideration is given to central city decline or inner city poverty. Gottmann's *Megalopolis* is a Manifest Destiny for postwar metropolitan America.

Gottmann's work was enormously influential. Based on the great success of his 1961 book, the term *megalopolis* entered the lexicon of urban studies. Four strands of subsequent work can be identified. First, the study prompted more detailed studies of the northeastern region (e.g., Alexander 1967; Borchert 1992; Pell 1966; Putnam 1975; Taeuber and Taeuber 1964). Weller (1967), for example, found scant evidence of increasing intermetropolitan division of labor and questioned the validity of the megalopolis as a new community form. There were many such studies that tested the validity of megalopolis as an organizing structure for understanding the sociospatial organization of cities. Many critics pointed to the considerable gaps in the urban fabric between Washington and Baltimore and derided the idea of a continuous urban region. Peter Hall questioned whether the term was a "convenient fiction, a tool for analysis or has it a deeper function or physical reality?" (Hall 1973, 46). Although the concept is still used occasionally—see for example the paper by Morrill (2006)—it fell out of favor as a tool for analyzing the Northeast.

Second, Gottmann's book initiated analyses of large city regions around the world (Wade 1969). In a typical work stimulated by Gottmann's writing, Chauncy Harris (1982) identifies the Tokaido megalopolis as the principal urban region of Japan. Such approaches continue today, reinvigorated by the sense that the processes of globalization are most vividly embodied in selected giant urban regions (Short 2004). When Scott (2001) uses the phrase "globalizing city region," he is in effect adopting a more recent version of megalopolis.

Third, the term also became a normative construct, something to avoid through strategic public policies. Osborn and Whittick (1963), for example, argue the case for "New Towns" as a way to avoid *megalopolis.* An extensive study of land-use planning in Britain was published in two volumes as *The Containment of Urban England,* with its first volume subtitled *Megalopolis Denied,* to refer to the fact that stringent planning controls averted the fate of the urbanized Northeast (Hall 1973). The term continues to be used as a journalistic device in contentious debates about urban growth and land use. Two more recent examples include a description of the area from San Clemente to Bakersfield in California as a "150-mile megalopolis of overpriced homes on postage-stamp lots dotted with shopping centers and mini-malls" (Anonymous 2003) and a depiction of central Texas in the midfuture as "a megalopolis of 2.5 million people" (Schwartz 2003). In current journalistic usage, *megalopolis* is often used to describe the unappealing endpoint of uncontrolled urban sprawl. Debates on New Urbanism and "smart growth," for example, are often framed as a way to avoid megalopolis.

Fourth, the term entered the English language as the name for any big city region. Even the briefest Web search reveals the regular use of the term in the popular press, from *The Economist* ("Brazil's Troubled Megalopolis") and *The New York Times* ("Open Space for a Crowded Megalopolis") to articles in such varied academic journals as *Ekistics* ("The Yangtze Delta Megalopolis") and *The Journal of Urban Economics* ("A Modeling of Megalopolis Formation"). In both academic articles and journalistic pieces, the term is used to add a dramatic flourish to urban commentaries. In recent years there has been a revival of interest in the idea of a megalopolitan geography. The Regional Plan Association, the Department of City and Regional Planning at the University of Pennsylvania, and the Lincoln Institute of Land Policy have all either sponsored or published work in the field. Carbonell and Yaro (2005) and Lang and Dhavale (2005a), for example, identify megalopolitan regions in the United States.

Gottmann produced other books. A sample of his later works is available in Gottmann and Harper (1990), but he is best known for *Megalopolis*. In 1986, on the occasion of the 25th anniversary of the book's publication, he was invited by the University of Maryland and the Smithsonian to reflect on the region a quarter-century later. In the subsequent monograph Gottmann notes the continuing concentration of population and the decentralization of diverse activities within the region. He repeats his idea that the region is an incubator of new trends and maintains his optimistic account of the region as a place for "opportunities favoring innovations, experimentations, cross-fertilization of knowledge and ideas" (Gottmann 1987).

Megalopolis is now a working definition of the urbanized Northeast to mid-Atlantic corridor, a generic term still used for identifying large urban regions around the world and describing the inevitable consequence of unabated sprawl. In this book I will use the capitalized version to refer to the urbanized northeastern seaboard of the United States and the lowercase form to refer to the generic term.

MEGALOPOLIS REDEFINED

Gottmann provided the organizing idea, but it is difficult to build directly on his actual definition of Megalopolis, since it is neither consistent nor clear. Although the first map in his 1957 paper uses the counties identi-fied in Bogue's 1951 report, subsequent maps in the paper have a different demarcation. I have identified at least six variants of the region used in his 1961 book. He excluded all of Maine and Vermont when writing about manufacturing, but when writing about agriculture, he included one and sometimes two counties in Maine and four counties in Vermont. Certain counties in New York, Virginia, Pennsylvania, Vermont, Maine, New Hamp-shire, and West Virginia appear and then disappear as his cartographic rep-resentation keeps changing. A map of forested areas by counties excludes all of Vermont and Maine and includes counties in New Hampshire, but a map of wooded land on farms shows four counties in Vermont, seven in New Hampshire, and one in Maine. A map of bank deposits by county excludes all of Vermont but shows six counties in New Hampshire and two in Maine. And when he employs spatial data, it is never exactly clear what precise definition of the region he is using. Gottmann provided the big idea but no consistent demarcation or empirical base to build upon. No defini-tive list of counties is ever presented in his article or book, thus requiring that a more robust set of criteria for Megalopolis be constructed.

In this study I will use the metric of contiguous metropolitan counties. The U.S. Census Bureau defines "metropolitan statistical area" (MSA) as a central city with a minimum population of 50,000 and surrounding counties that are functionally linked to the city through levels of commut-ing, population density, and population growth. Counties with a "high degree of social and economic integration"—to use the formal Census definition—with the city are, by definition, part of an MSA. From 1950 to 1990, one of the many standard measures was the level of commuting: if a county sent more than 15 percent of its total commuters to the central city, it was considered part of the MSA. In 2000 the threshold was raised to 25 percent.

There are also two other metropolitan designations in addition to MSAs. Consolidated metropolitan statistical areas (CMSAs) fulfill the same re-quirements of an MSA but have a total population of at least 1 million. Primary metropolitan statistical areas (PMSAs) are the building blocks of CMSAs; a PMSA consists of a large urbanized county or cluster of coun-ties at its core and total population of at least 1 million.

Recently, the Census Bureau changed its terminology and designation and now employs "micropolitan statistical area" to refer to a place with an urban cluster of at least 10,000 and a population no greater than 50,000. Together, the metropolitan and micropolitan statistical areas are referred to as core-based statistical areas (CBSAs). Another recent change is the use

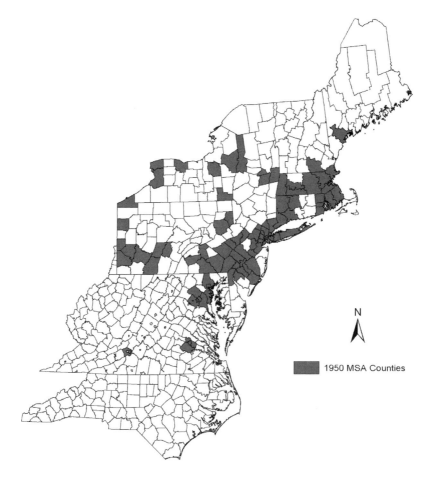

Figure 2-1.   Metropolitan Counties in the Northeast, 1950

of "combined statistical areas," which are aggregates of adjacent metropolitan or micropolitan statistical areas that are linked by commuting ties. This new, more flexible designation has been used only since 2003. Because micropolitan areas are insignificant in Megalopolis and since many of the data reported here predate this new terminology and designation, I will continue to use only MSA, PMSA, and CMSA. However, analyses of future census data are more likely to employ combined statistical areas.

For our purposes, then, the Census Bureau already identifies counties in the orbit of an urban center. We will define counties within MSAs, CMSAs, and PMSAs as metropolitan counties. Using counties has both advantages and disadvantages. On the one hand, they are units of observation that remain consistent over the 50-year period from 1950 to 2000 and thus allow

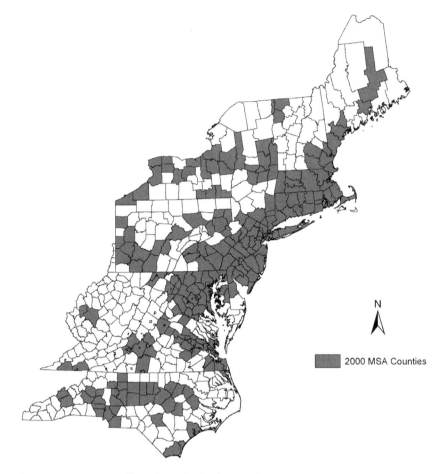

Figure 2-2.   Metropolitan Counties in the Northeast, 2000

an easier longitudinal comparison. They are also administrative units with a political reality and planning purpose. They contain the cities of Baltimore and Philadelphia as well as the traditional areas of county jurisdiction. Counties are irregular in size but provide a consistent frame of reference. On the other hand, they are large units that are not homogeneous. They range in population from almost 2.5 million people in King's County, New York, to just over 19,000 in Kent County, Maryland; in area from 1,513 square miles in Worcester County, Massachusetts, to tiny 2-square-mile Falls Church, Virginia; and in population density from the teeming 66,835 people per square mile in New York County to the scattered 69 people per square mile living in Androscoggin, Maine.

Figure 2-3.   Major Cities in Megalopolis

The number of metropolitan counties increased over the period 1950 to 2000 for the whole region (Figures 2-1 and 2-2), and they began to spread outside the core corridor. In 1950 North Carolina had none and Virginia, only a few; metropolitan counties were concentrated instead in the eastern seaboard and the inland industrial areas, such as Pittsburgh. Even the areas that Gottmann identified as Megalopolis showed gaps: there was no continuous metropolitan coverage in the core area with, for example, four nonmetro counties in Connecticut (Tolland, Windham, New London, and Middlesex). In 1950, then, Megalopolis was still embryonic. Over the 50-year period there was a substantial infilling in the core area along the northeastern seaboard to create a continuous coverage of metro counties from Maine to Virginia, an extension of metro counties into formerly more rural areas adjoining metro counties, and the creation of new metro areas in southern Virginia and the Charlotte-to-Raleigh area in North Carolina.

From 1950 to 2000 there was metropolitan consolidation, metropolitan extension, and the birth of entirely new metropolitan areas.

The next question is where to draw the boundary. Since I wanted to maintain the notion of a coherent, consolidated region, I made two exceptions to the metro status. Kent County and Talbot County, both in Maryland, were not metropolitan counties in 2000 but were effectively surrounded by other metropolitan counties. Using contiguous 2000 metropolitan counties as the single criterion would result in a Megalopolis with thin strands connecting to western Pennsylvania and upstate and western New York. The decision of where to draw the final demarcation between contiguous metro counties shown in Figure 2-3 was subjective. Lines could have been drawn to include the Albany metro area in New York and the Richmond metro area in Virginia. Ultimately the final demarcation represents a judgment call.

The area that I have identified as Megalopolis consists of 52,310 square miles stretching across 12 states, the District of Columbia, and 124 counties (Figure 2-4). In 1950 Megalopolis consisted of 32 separate metropolitan areas. By 2000 the region contained 12 MSAs and 32 PMSAs that had merged into four CMSAs, reflecting the growing interconnection between metropolitan areas in this region (Tables 2-1 and 2-2). Megalopolis is now one extended urban region strung along the four CMSAs of Boston, New York, Philadelphia, and Washington-Baltimore.

The display of data for such a complex area creates difficulties within the confines of a single text. The reader is directed to the electronic atlas of Megalopolis at http://www.umbc.edu/ges/student_projects/digital_atlas/instructions.htm where more than 60 maps of social and economic data are cartographically presented. This is an indispensable source of information that complements and contextualizes the discussion in this book.

LIQUID LIFE, LIQUID CITY

At this stage I want to introduce the notion of a liquid city. I draw upon the observations of sociologist Zygmunt Bauman, whose book *Liquid Life* (2005) describes the precariousness of life under conditions of constant uncertainty. Bauman uses the term to refer to time and the question of identity in a rapidly changing world, but I think it is also appropriate to use with reference to space and the incoherence of the built environment. Metropolitan growth has a liquid quality; it is constantly moving over the landscape, here

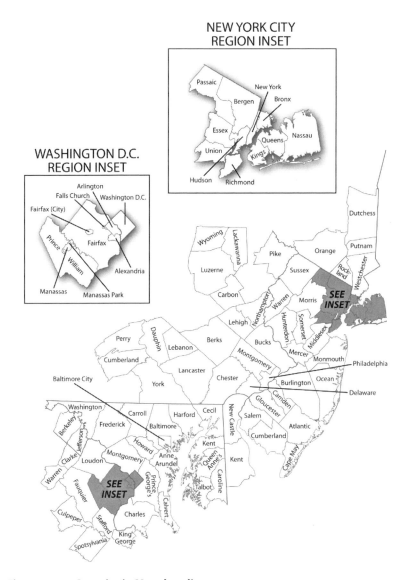

Figure 2-4.   Counties in Megalopolis

in torrents, there in rivulets, elsewhere in steady drips, but always in the viscous manner of a semisolid, semiliquid, half-permanent, yet constantly changing phenomenon. Metropolitan growth possesses an unstable quality that flows over political boundaries, seeps across borders, and transcends tight spatial demarcations; it is a process not a culmination, always in motion, rarely at rest. Megalopolis is a large liquid metropolis whose boundary demarcation is always provisional. It is a giant metropolitan region always

Table 2-1.   Primary Metropolitan Statistical Areas in Megalopolis, 2000

	State(s)	Population
Allentown-Bethlehem-Easton MSA	PA	637,958
Atlantic–Cape May PMSA	NJ	354,878
Baltimore PMSA	MD	2,552,994
Barnstable-Yarmouth MSA	MA	162,582
Bergen-Passaic PMSA	NJ	1,373,167
Boston PMSA	MA, NH	3,406,829
Bridgeport PMSA	CT	459,479
Brockton PMSA	MA	255,459
Danbury PMSA	CT	217,980
Dutchess County PMSA	NY	280,150
Fitchburg-Leominster PMSA	MA	142,284
Hagerstown PMSA	MD	131,923
Hartford MSA	CT	1,183,110
Jersey City PMSA	NJ	608,975
Lancaster MSA	PA	470,658
Lawrence PMSA	MA, NH	396,230
Lowell PMSA	MA, NH	301,686
Manchester PMSA	NH	198,378
Middlesex-Somerset-Hunterdon PMSA	NJ	1,169,641
Monmouth-Ocean PMSA	NJ	1,126,217
Nashua PMSA	NH	190,949
Nassau-Suffolk PMSA	NY	2,753,913
New Bedford PMSA	MA	175,198
New Haven–Meriden PMSA	CT	542,149
New London–Norwich MSA	CT, RI	293,566
New York PMSA	NY	9,314,235
Newark PMSA	NJ	2,032,989
Newburgh PMSA	NY, PA	387,669
Philadelphia PMSA	PA, NJ	5,100,931
Pittsfield MSA	MA	84,699
Portland MSA	ME	243,537
Portsmouth-Rochester PMSA	NH, MA	240,698
Providence–Fall River–Warwick MSA	RI, MA	1,188,613
Reading MSA	PA	373,638
Scranton–Wilkes-Barre–Hazleton MSA	PA	624,776
Springfield MSA	MA	591,932
Stamford-Norwalk PMSA	CT	353,556
Trenton PMSA	NJ	350,761
Vineland-Millville-Bridgeton PMSA	NJ	146,438
Washington, DC PMSA	DC, MD, VA, WV	4,923,153
Waterbury PMSA	CT	228,984
Wilmington-Newark PMSA	DE, MD	586,216
Worcester PMSA	MA, CT	511,389
York MSA	PA	381,751

Table 2-2.   Consolidated Metropolitan Statistical Areas in Megalopolis, 2000

	States	Population
New York–Northern New Jersey–Long Island	NY, NJ, CT, PA	21,199,865
Washington-Baltimore	DC, MD, VA, WV	7,608,070
Philadelphia–Wilmington–Atlantic City	PA, NJ, DE, MD	6,188,463
Boston-Worcester-Lawrence	MA, NH, ME, CT	5,819,100

in a state of becoming as well as being. Like any solid lines around liquid phenomena, the limits of the region I identify are an approximation, the uncertain fixing of a moving object.

I employ the term *liquid city* to grasp the nature of this urban change. Gottmann's 1957 paper used *Megalopolis* in recognition of the spread and transformation of the urban region beyond the narrow city boundaries and even the wider city region to a spatially extensive, interconnected system of multiple metropolitan areas. In 1991 Joel Garreau coined the term *Edge City* to refer to the centrifugal spread of population, office space, and retail establishments. He suggested that new concentrations could be identified at specific edges. In 2003 in *Edgeless Cities* Robert Lang challenged this notion and wrote of an elusive metropolis with few sharp edges. The evolution of terms reflects the nature of urban change, and thus in 2007 we have *liquid city.* The term is useful, but it does need to be applied with caution. It does not, for example, imply that all is in flux. Fixed and frozen elements remain, such as elements of the built form and the persistent patterns of segregation, but they are constantly assailed by change and movement. Large clumps of capital investment such as motorways and airports remain fixed in place, affecting subsequent flows of investment and movement. But flows there are, along with tensions between the fixed nature of the city and urban movements, especially the continual centrifugal forces in Megalopolis. Fixity parries with flow in a constant dialectic as flows produce new places of fixed investment and concentration that in turn are undermined by new flows. Structure and process, solid and liquid, stasis and flow continually interact, and *liquid city* highlights the more dynamic element of the dialectic.

My spatial definition of Megalopolis compares closely to previous studies. Figure 2-5 juxtaposes the present Megalopolis with the 1951 study and the largest of Gottmann's demarcations. The 1951 study is a prescient prediction of future developments, a testament to the robust nature of the 1951 government survey. There is also remarkable similarity with the Gottmann demarcation. Although there are some minor discrepancies at the periphery—a function of subsequent expansion for counties excluded by

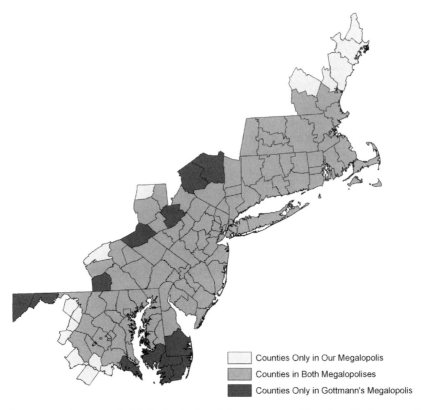

Figure 2-5.   Gottmann's Original (1951) and Contemporary Megalopolis, Compared

Gottmann, and perhaps an overbounding for some counties included by Gottmann—these occur in places where the liquidity of the metropolis is difficult to ascertain with pinpoint precision. Let me salute the quality of the earlier studies, the careful anatomy of the core in the 1951 study, and the more expansive area coverage adopted by Gottmann; they managed to capture very early on the coherent aspects of the fluid city.

Having defined the region, what does it mean? In what sense is Megalopolis a region? It is clearly not a single political jurisdiction, ranging as it does over different states, counties, and municipalities. Neither is it a term in common popular usage. And neither is it a source of identity. People who live in the region do not refer to themselves as residents of Megalopolis. Their identities are linked to a scale well below this giant region. But this disparity between the lived urban experience of individuals on the one hand and the brute existence of a region of contiguous metropolitan counties on the other raises an important issue. The end result of myriad individual actions, investment decisions, and political choices is the collective, unforeseen creation of a giant urban region larger than our capacity to humanize it and greater than our imagination to conceptualize it. Megalopolis stands as a testimony to the unplanned, collective end point of individual everyday decisions. When households move to the suburbs of Washington, Baltimore, New York, and Boston, and stores locate along strips leading away from the city, collectively they are creating a vast urban network that covers the land with a liquid metropolis. We still have a sense that a city should be bounded, comprehensible, with boundaries that we can encompass in our everyday lives and conceptual models. The sheer extent of Megalopolis questions all of these assumptions. The liquid metropolis has oozed beyond our ken. Megalopolis takes us beyond formal city boundaries, everyday lived experiences, and common conceptions of the city, urban growth, and metropolitan frontiers. In a way it is also the product of the provisional, accidental, even surreal quality of the unplanned metropolis.

Michel de Certeau (1984) makes a distinction between strategies and tactics. *Strategy* refers to the spatial ordering of powerful interests; *tactics* refers to appropriations and transgressions. Through tactics, the strategies of power can be undermined and appropriated. Life in the city is conceptualized as reinforcing both the spatial strategies of the official city and the tactical appropriation of the everyday resistances. De Certeau's work is enormously influential in its articulation of the need to connect the official and the everyday, the compliance and resistances embodied in the space-time paths we make across the urban built form, and the routes we weave across urban social space. But it takes us only so far, and Megalopolis highlights the limits of this conceptualization. Beyond strategy and tactics are unforeseen consequences—new spatial forms of the city that are neither strategic nor tactical, but unplanned, unimagined, and unforeseen. Megalopolis is at the very limit of our understanding, just beyond our capacity to theorize it as more than a liquid concept. Megalopolis is at the outer limits of the definition of a liquid metropolis.

To make some sense of the issue of whether Megalopolis exists, which I will treat as an epistemological rather than an ontological question, we can draw upon the works of Karl Marx, who made a distinction between *a class in itself* and *a class for itself*. A class *in* itself is shaped by economic and historic conditions, but for a class *for* itself to emerge, there needs to be a conscious sense of shared identity and an appreciation of a shared fate. Similarly, we can identify urban regions in themselves. However, many things militate against their becoming regions for themselves; political fragmentation, the legacy of separate identities, and the tendency for identities to be more local and national than regional. While economic forces are creating a region in itself, many things operate in the political and cultural realms to stop the creation of regional consciousnesses. The major cities of Megalopolis, for example, have separate regional news stations and different sports teams. In terms of baseball allegiances, we move from north to south through the territories of the Boston Red Sox, New York Yankees and Mets, Philadelphia Phillies, Baltimore Orioles, and Washington Nationals. In football terms, traveling south to north is to cross the fierce rivalries between the Redskins, Ravens, Eagles, Jets, and Giants to the New England Patriots. Local school districts, different states and counties, metro TV markets, and fierce sports rivalries all work to suppress the creation of an urban regional consciousness. Megalopolis is a region in itself but not a region for itself.

This chapter has sought to provide a provisional definition of Megalopolis at the beginning of the 21st century. It is pitched at a general level. Let me end with a more human-scale story told by the journalist Alex MacGillis (2006) that touches on the creation of a region in itself without the generation of a region for itself.

Every working day a group of eight men assemble at around 3:50 A.M. in Luray in Page County, Virginia. At 4 A.M. they leave in a bus that takes them 77 miles north along Route 340 and west on Interstate 66 through the expanding suburbs to George Mason University. The men work in the physical plant shop of the university from 6 A.M. until 2.30 P.M., when they begin their long journey back to Page County. They are not long-distance commuters who have moved out for more space and cheaper houses. They are long-term residents of Luray who have seen economic opportunities in their small town dwindle as the printing plant and the tannery closed. They need employment. George Mason University, on the other hand, needs workers and can pay only around $33,000 a year, a wage that is half the living wage for a family in Fairfax County. The university uses six vans to ferry in workers from far afield. One of the workers, Sam Dean, has to travel 25 miles just to get to the early morning pickup point; only 10 hours after getting home from work, he leaves again. Page County does not even qualify under the contiguous metropolitan county rule that I use to designate counties in Megalopolis. It is off the map yet still linked by complex patterns of commuting. Around Megalopolis the complex patterns of linkages as exemplified between Page County and George Mason University connect a dispersed and liquid metropolis.

The mathematician John von Neumann once remarked that we never understand things, we just get used to them. We have gotten used to giant urban regions with their networks that eddy and flow through cities and suburbs across hundreds of miles. Perhaps it is also time to understand them.

CHAPTER THREE

POPULATION DISPERSAL
AND CONCENTRATION

I n 1950 Megalopolis had a population of almost 32 million people. One in four of all U.S. residents lived in this region. By 2000 the population had increased to almost 49 million (Table 3-1). In absolute terms the area saw an increase of almost 17 million people, but the Megalopolis share of the total U.S. population fell from almost 21 percent to just over 17 percent. This change can be read in a number of ways. On the one hand, the numbers indicate a relative shift in national population away from Megalopolis. The economic geography of postwar growth, a shift from the frostbelt of the Midwest and Northeast to the sunbelt of the West and South, shrunk the relative share of the population of Megalopolis. There has been a differential rate of metropolitan growth across the country. Between 1980 and 2000, while the New York and Boston consolidated metropolitan statistical areas (CMSAs) grew by approximately 10 percent, to 21.20 million and 5.81 million, respectively, the Los Angeles CMSA grew by 29.7 percent, to 16.37 million. The United States shifted its center of economic gravity and population distribution toward the South and West, and Megalopolis no longer holds the position of dominance noted by Gottmann. The declining proportion of national population is an indicator of

Table 3-1.   Population Change in Megalopolis

	1950	2000
Population	31,924,488	48,720,108
Percentage of U.S. population	20.9	17.3
Population per square mile	610.2	931.3
U.S. population per square mile	42.6	80.5

the region's decline in national importance. The region neither dominates the national economy nor shapes the national identity to the extent that it did in 1950.

On the other hand, this small area of just over 52,000 square miles, with only 1.4 percent of the national land surface, still contains more than 17.3 percent, or about one in six persons, of the nation's population. Despite the national redistribution of the U.S. population, Megalopolis remains a significant center. In 1950 the average population density was 610 persons per square mile; by 2000 this had increased to 931 persons per square mile. Although its national importance has declined, the region continues to boast a significant population concentration at densities much higher than the national average. Megalopolis is still the largest single concentration of population in the United States.

The environmental impact of this population is enormous: more people driving more cars to more places; more people running dishwashers, flushing toilets, and taking showers; more people in more and ever bigger houses. Megalopolis is subject to the constant, mounting stress of a rising population with an ever-growing list of needs and desires.

Consider automobiles. Applying the standard estimates of one car for every five people in 1950 and one car for every two people in 2000 yields a total of 6.4 million cars in 1950 and 24.25 million cars in 2000. In the same surface area, the number of cars has almost quadrupled. And this total does not include the buses, cars, and trucks passing through this region from the outside. There are now, at the very lowest estimate, more than 24 million autos releasing exhaust, needing roads, and requiring parking spaces. The landscape has been redesigned to give drivers the space and freedom to move throughout the region.

And water usage: in 1950 daily per capita water withdrawals for the United States totaled 1,027 gallons; by 1995 (the latest available statistic) this figure had increased to 1,500 gallons. In Megalopolis, not only has the population increased, but so has water usage—by 50 percent per head. These figures need to be treated with some care: national statistics tend to overestimate rates of withdrawal, since per capita water usage is less in urban areas than in rural areas. However, although the absolute amounts are only very rough estimates, their direction is clear. Total water withdrawal increased in the region by more than 150 percent from 1950 to 2000.

A similar picture emerges for municipal solid waste generation. In 2000 each American generated 4.3 pounds per day. By the end of the 20th century, the population of Megalopolis generated approximately 4.8 pounds per person per day for a grand total of 100,000 *tons* of garbage per day. Consider the case of New York City, which each day generates approximately 12,000 tons of municipal waste and an equal amount of waste collected by private companies. Since the closing of the Fresh Kills landfill in Staten Island in 2002, the city now has an elaborate system for the transfer and disposal of the municipal waste. Trash is collected and hauled by 550 trash trucks to transfer stations in the city and New Jersey and then transported for incineration in Newark and dumping in landfills in Pennsylvania, New Jersey, and as far south as Virginia. Trash trucks have increased congestion and raised the pollution levels along such routes as Canal Street by as much as 17 percent. In some of the receiving areas, taxes from landfill companies pay as much as 40 percent of the school budget (Lipton 2001). Megalopolis is one giant waste-generating, waste-disposal region.

Whatever the measure, increasing population growth in association with increased affluence and spiraling consumption is expanding the environmental footprint and straining natural systems. Close to 50 million people with the greatest environmental impact per head in the history of the world now live in Megalopolis.

POPULATION DENSITY

Population density is a good measure of the "weight" of population; the higher the density, the greater the human impress on the land, the more marked the human transformation of the landscape. Population density is a useful indicator of the collective human impact on the environment.

The Northeast–mid-Atlantic is the most densely settled region in the country. Figures 3-1 and 3-2 plot the population density over the period 1950 to 2000. The pattern shows a thickening density in the core corridor of Megalopolis and a slow spread of increasing density across the whole region. The liquid city spills out over the entire region with only the more inaccessible parts of Maine, Virginia, West Virginia, Pennsylvania, and upstate New York remaining relatively untouched.

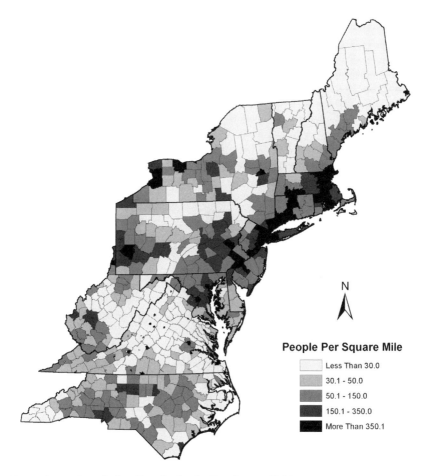

Figure 3-1.   Population Density in the Northeast, 1950

Within this region of almost 49 million people, a central spine of especially dense population runs from Washington through Philadelphia and the counties of New Jersey up to New York; it thins and then thickens again around Boston. This spine includes such counties as Camden, New Jersey, with a population of 508,932, and Middlesex, New Jersey, with 750,762. The largest counties in terms of population are in the New York City area: Kings has a population of 2.4 million and Queens, 2.2 million. The small-population counties, such as King George, Virginia, with 16,803 and Clarke, Virginia, with only 12,652, are on the fringes. At the center of Megalopolis is, in U.S. terms, an astonishing concentration of population, the densest in the nation.

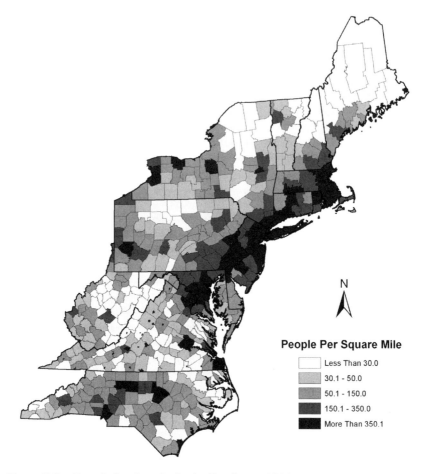

People Per Square Mile

	Less Than 30.0
	30.1 - 50.0
	50.1 - 150.0
	150.1 - 350.0
	More Than 350.1

Figure 3-2.   Population Density in the Northeast, 2000

Megalopolis is the most densely populated area of the most densely settled region of the country. The figure for population density in Megalopolis is more than 10 times the national figure. Whereas there are almost 80 people per square mile in the United States, there are almost 930 people per square mile in Megalopolis.

Significant variations within Megalopolis should be noted. Figures 3-3 and 3-4 give us a bird's-eye view of population density for 1950 and 2000. What stands out, quite literally, is the tower of enormous population density in New York City and the immediate surrounding area in 1950. Smaller areas of density are noticeable—the cities of Washington, Baltimore, Philadelphia, and Boston. The dominant pattern is of high-density cities surrounded by a flat plain of low density. Over the 50-year period, the towers

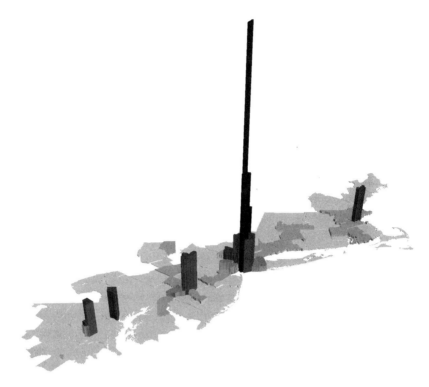

Figure 3-3.   Population Density in Megalopolis, 1950

of high population density, apart from New York City, shrink as the population flows out from the cities into the surrounding areas. Figures 3-3 and 3-4 provide a striking visual image of the liquidity of the city as the towers of population ooze into the surrounding areas.

Megalopolis now has a spine of very high population density along the urban corridor from Washington through Baltimore, Philadelphia, and New York to Boston. The highest figures are in New York City, where densities reach a staggering 66,835 persons per square mile (ppsm), one of the highest densities anywhere in the country. Because of its economic vitality, New York has retained its high population density long after many other U.S. cities have lost population. In population density, New York City resembles European cities more than any other U.S. city. Counties in the New York metro area, including Kings (34,723 ppsm), Bronx (31,730 ppsm), and Queens (20,453 ppsm), also show high-density figures. The other cities in the central corridor have lower yet still significant peaks of density, including Washington (9,378 ppsm), Baltimore (8,039 ppsm), and Philadelphia (1,241 ppsm).

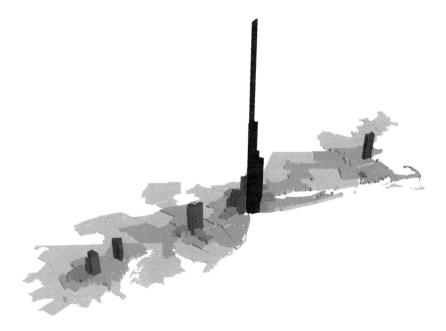

Figure 3-4.   Population Density in Megalopolis, 2000

The areas around these major cities that have experienced significant suburbanization of population and employment are at the next level of high population density. Counties such as Baltimore County, around Baltimore City, and Middlesex County, around Boston, all have density figures of more than 1,000 ppsm. As more people and jobs leave the central city, the suburban areas have increased in population density. The resulting densities are not so high as to sustain public transport, but enough to create increased traffic and the transformation of agricultural and rural land to suburban sprawl.

The areas of lowest population density are situated away from the central spine and especially in the more peripheral areas of Megalopolis. Clarke County in Virginia, for example, is on the southern fringe of the region, more than a two hours' commute from Washington. With only 12,652 people spread over its 177 square miles, the county's density figure is only 71 ppsm. Densities dissolve at the edges of Megalopolis in areas farthest from the major metro areas.

CREATING THE LIQUID METROPOLIS

The liquidity of the region—the flow of population and economic activities away from the dense central cities—is one of the most significant features of Megalopolis. People and jobs have moved away from the central cities toward the suburbs, transforming dense urban agglomerations into a more dispersed metropolitan region.

There are many reasons for the spread of the population. In this chapter I concentrate on the role of government. An important infrastructural prerequisite for this spread away from central cities was the construction of the interstate highway system. In 1944 Congress earmarked 25 percent of all federal highway funds for road construction in urban areas. Half the cost of urban highways was to be paid by the federal government, but even with this subsidy, building new roads in urban areas was expensive because of the high costs of land and construction. The big prompt came with the Federal-Aid Highway Act of 1956, when the federal government agreed to pay 90 percent of the costs of interstate highway construction. This subsidy enabled planners to lay highways through central cities and out to distant suburbs and rural areas. The federal highway system thus encouraged the dispersal of low-density suburbia across the landscape into rural areas, where land prices were relatively low. The interstate highway system laid the routes for the centrifugal sifting of population. Federally funded roads allowed people to travel relatively easily across municipal boundaries. The federal highway construction program, especially by the late 1950s and 1960s, not only connected cities but also allowed commuters to travel into the cities from nearby (and eventually not-so-nearby) suburbs. The highways made it easier to live in one area and work in another. The huge road-building schemes created a metropolis of endless flows and mobility.

Megalopolis is crisscrossed with interstate highways that emerged under the federal legislation. The central north-south route, I-95, runs all the way down the east coast. Running east to west are a series of interstates beginning with 66 in the south of the region with the number increasing as we head north: I-70, I-76, I-78, I-80 (which runs 2,907 miles from New York City to San Francisco), I-84, and I-90 (which covers 3,081 miles from Boston to Seattle). Looping around the major cities are circular beltways, I-495 in Washington, I-695 in Baltimore, I-295 and I-476 encircling Philadelphia, I-287 around New York, and I-95 around Boston. Initially built as bypasses around the major cities, these loops are now concrete channels for metropolitan liquidity.

URBAN RENEWAL

Let us consider the underlying dynamics of the great suburban shift in terms of the more important push-and-pull factors shaped by public policies. The biggest push came from the federal government in the form of urban renewal. The central cities of Megalopolis lost much of their population and low-income housing stock with the urban renewal policies that were first formulated in the Housing Act of 1949. Under Title I of the 1949 act, the federal government paid for two-thirds of the cost of purchasing and clearing "blighted" housing. In today's dollars, the program cost almost $100 billion. By 1973, when the program officially ended, 2,000 individual projects had been undertaken covering 1,000 square miles of urban land; 600,000 units had been demolished and 2 million people displaced. The program that began with so much hope for the elimination of substandard housing ended up destroying communities, increasing segregation, and laying the basis for subsequent central city decline.

The initial plan was to demolish substandard housing, and legislation stipulated that for each unit of housing torn down, one should be rebuilt. In practice, local authorities and redevelopment agencies, strongly representing investors and downtown business interests, implemented the plans in favor of replacing low-income housing with tax-generating, commercial property. Thus a plan emanating from Washington to eliminate substandard housing soon was compromised at the local level by municipalities and redevelopment agencies following their own definitions of urban renewal. The 1954 Housing Act effectively turned the housing policy into a renewal policy. When implemented, the program involved a net loss of housing: four dwellings were demolished for every one built, and as low-rent homes were demolished and replaced by more expensive housing and by commercial developments, such as parking garages, hospitals, shopping centers, and office blocks, low-income families faced a tight housing market. The 1954 Housing Act was a highly regressive policy because housing market conditions deteriorated for the poorest while business interests received federal subsidization.

Throughout Megalopolis, the central areas of cities were remade in a vision that stressed mobility over community and the new over the old. Blocks were flattened, houses were destroyed, and communities were disrupted. Older structures were demolished to make way for the new. But something other than just old housing was lost. The wrecking ball destroyed the vitality of many central cities. Slums were demolished but so were vibrant neighborhoods, often replaced by sterile public spaces and vacant lots. Urban renewal eviscerated many of the central cities in Megalopolis.

Urban renewal was particularly devastating in Megalopolis because the housing stock was much older than in many other parts of the country and thus more susceptible to urban renewal. Most cities saw a net loss of dwellings and the construction of unfriendly urban spaces. Major projects took place in both large and small cities throughout Megalopolis. In the Fourth Street Redevelopment Project in Southwest Washington, 64 percent of the dwellings in the area were considered too dilapidated to repair and all were scheduled for demolition. The area contained many small businesses and homes for African Americans. Sam Berman, the executor of an estate that contained a small department store condemned under eminent domain by the public agency responsible for the project, went to court. The case finally ended up in the Supreme Court, which in its 1954 ruling *Berman v. Parker* sided with the public agency and the subsequent urban renewal that demolished the homes and business and replaced them with offices and residential and hotel complexes. Even the liberal Justice William O. Douglas ruled in favor of the agency, arguing that if owners were permitted to resist, "integrated plans for redevelopment would suffer greatly." The Supreme Court ruling also had wider implications, as it allowed the use of eminent domain for the compulsory purchase of private land by a public agency and its subsequent transfer to a private corporation. The ruling opened the door to large-scale urban renewal across the central cities of the nation.

The cities of Megalopolis were particularly affected by urban renewal. In terms of urban renewal grants per capita, Baltimore ranked first in the nation, followed by New York. Boston was eighth and Philadelphia was ninth. Urban renewal programs demolished not only substandard housing but also destroyed sound housing and functioning neighborhoods. Almost 40 percent of the demolished dwellings were classified as sound. Studies of relocated families paint a depressing picture. Gans (1962), for example, examined the fate of families relocated from Boston's West End, a 38-block, 41-acre neighborhood of some 8,500 people that was demolished in 1958–1959. Luxury apartments were built on the ruins of the low-rent, low-rise Italian neighborhood. The study shows that for most of the relocated people, housing costs had increased while their housing quality was often only marginally improved. Gans lived in the area for eight months in 1957–1958 and did not romanticize it; he described the West End as "a run-down area of people struggling with the problems of low-income, poor education and related difficulties." But he called it "by and large a good place to live" and painted a picture of a vibrant community where life in the neighborhood revolved more around family connections than around educational attainment or career aspirations. A tight society was making a life in difficult circumstances in a low-rent area, but the designation "slum" justified its destruction.

Urban renewal also affected the smaller cities of Megalopolis. Portland, Maine, like many cities in the 1950s and 1960s, was losing population and business. A "general neighborhood renewal plan" was promoted as a way to revive the downtown, involving the construction of the I-295 spur and the creation of new arterial routes. The plan also demanded the destruction of 1,200 dwelling units, the severing of neighborhoods, and the loss of parkland as well as the demolition of the historic Union Station and post office. In Portland, as in other cities, the destruction prompted a protest and resistance. Greater Portland Landmarks was created in 1963 to protest the destruction of historic buildings, and its actions softened the demolition focus of urban renewal and saved many of the older buildings and structures in the city. As in Portland, preservation groups and community activists mobilized in cities throughout Megalopolis and across the country to shift the direction of urban redevelopment policy.

PUBLIC HOUSING

The 1949 Housing Act, the same act that introduced urban renewal, also made provision for public housing. Under it, 135,000 to 200,000 public housing units would be built each year until 1960 to meet the demands of low-income households for housing. Of the projected total of 2 million units, however, only 650,000 had been built by 1962. The 1949 act emphasized local voluntary involvement, but because suburban municipalities did not want public housing, almost none was built outside the central cities. Moreover, the housing that was built was confined to existing slum areas, further stigmatizing public housing. In the large cities of Megalopolis, urban renewal involved the destruction of dense neighborhoods and their replacement with public housing projects of high-rise towers that quickly became warehouses for the poor, housing mostly racial minorities. Large modernist blocks, often called "the projects," dominated public housing construction. Poorly maintained and shoddily constructed, they became dumping grounds for the poor, emblematic of poverty and despair.

Baltimore is a typical example. The city's ambitious public housing building program began with Lafayette Court, six 11-story towers, completed in

1954. In the same year the three-tower, 12-story Flag House was finished. In 1959 Lexington Terrace opened; it comprised one tower of 14 stories and four of 11 stories. Three years later the four 14-story buildings of George B. Murphy Homes opened their doors. Two more schemes were built in 1971 and 1976, one a 22-story tower and the other a 20-story building. All but one of the developments were in the inner city. By the early 1990s the buildings were vertical slums and highly unpopular: they were concrete warehouses for the black poor; 98 percent of the residents of Lafayette Court were black and 86 percent were earning less than the poverty level. Things became so bad in Baltimore and across the nation that cities eagerly adopted a new federal program, Hope VI, to demolish the towers. Lafayette Court was blown up in August 1995, Lexington fell in July 1996, and Murphy Homes in July 1999. The demolition of Flag House in February 2001 marked the literal end of high-rise public housing in Baltimore.

SUBURBAN GROWTH

Although there had been suburbanization before World War II, it was limited in size and scale. Suburbs were essentially appendages to a central city. The early suburbs were often new housing developments within the city boundaries. After World War II, suburbanization extended beyond traditional municipal boundaries, creating new metropolitan forms. There were powerful forces pulling people and business to the suburbs; these included the federal encouragement of suburban owner-occupation, changes in technology, and racial politics.

The federal government fostered suburban growth by promoting suburban homeownership and highway construction. Suburbanization began in the New Deal with a Roosevelt administration eager to stimulate employment at a time of mass unemployment. The Federal Housing Administration (FHA) was established in 1934 to insure mortgages. Home loans thus became safe investments, the risk underwritten by the financial weight and authority of the federal government. Bankers were now willing to lend money to house buyers, who in turn purchased homes that required workers to build them. Government involvement helped lower interest payments, reduce down payments, and lengthen the repayment period. Prior to FHA, buyers often needed to put down 50 percent of the loan and pay the loan within five years. Homeownership had thus been restricted to the affluent.

A typical FHA loan, in contrast, required just 10 percent down with 30 years to pay. These requirements soon became standard industry practice.

The FHA program had dramatic effects in both the short and the long term. It immediately stimulated the production of housing. The number of housing starts, only 332,000 in 1937, almost doubled to 619,000 by 1941. In the years between 1944 and 1965, one-quarter to one-third of all mortgages were either FHA or the similar Veterans Administration (VA) mortgage program. The VA program was part of the 1944 GI Bill, crafted to provide educational and housing opportunities to service families. The VA mortgage program was similar to the FHA scheme. By 1972 the FHA-VA programs had helped 11 million families to purchase houses, revolutionized the home loan industry, and made homeownership more accessible to a wider range of the population. The FHA-VA programs were a major factor in creating a large new class of homeowners.

The programs stimulated suburbanization because they had strict lending guidelines that favored the building of single-family homes in suburban areas. The most favorable loans were made available only for new construction. Loans for improvement to existing dwellings were smaller and of a shorter duration. This bias worked against older, inner-city areas. The programs were also racially biased, especially from 1934 to 1965. Between 1945 and 1959, for example, less than 2 percent of all FHA-VA mortgages went to African Americans. The FHA-VA made few loans within minority neighborhoods. Loan guarantees were based on appraisals that were explicitly biased toward all-white, single-family neighborhoods and against minority neighborhoods in central cities. Almost 90 percent of loans went to the suburbs. FHA made suburbs less the preserve of the affluent and extended the suburban experience to middle- and lower-income households, but it also supported the white flight to the suburbs and the racial segregation of suburbia. The racial divide between central city and suburbia is in part the direct result of decades of government lending patterns.

THE CASE OF LEVITTOWN

The archetypal postwar suburb was Levittown. The name comes from two brothers, William and Alfred Levitt, who had been house builders since 1929. Like most builders of the time, they concentrated on small-scale developments for affluent buyers. In 1941 they received a government contract to build more than 2,000 houses for workers in Norfolk, Virginia. There they learned the techniques of rapid mass production that they would later use to great effect.

The two brothers purchased 4,000 acres of potato farms 25 miles east of Manhattan on Long Island and began building homes in July 1947. They standardized house building to a set of assembly procedures. A concrete slab was laid, and in 27 distinct steps the house was built out of composition sheetrock and plywood. The Levitts turned house building from a craft industry to mass assembly production and erected up to 30 homes from preassembled materials in a single day. The result was relatively cheap housing, built to basic standard designs; a typical house sold for $7,990. For many middle-income Americans with FHA-VA mortgages, it was cheaper to buy than to rent. Eventually, 17,400 houses were built in Levittown and the new suburb became home to 82,000 people. But it wasn't open to everyone. Racial covenants in the sales contracts barred resale to blacks, and the suburb remained all white until the 1960s.

Other Levittowns were built in Pennsylvania and New Jersey, and many other builders soon adopted the Levitt construction techniques. There was a ready market for the mass-produced houses because of the FHA and VA mortgage programs.

GOVERNMENT STIMULATION

There were other government stimulants to suburbanization. Federal tax rules favored owner occupation. Mortgage interest payments were and continue to be tax deductible. By the mid-1960s homeownership deductions were worth around $7 billion and by 1984 amounted to $53 billion. Low-income renters receive no parallel tax break. Tax expenditures are skewed toward owner-occupiers. Under a 1951 federal tax law people did not have to pay capital gains on any profits on their home if the money was used to buy another house. This was a fiscal incentive to the upward spiral in average home size and cost.

Tax breaks did not just aid in the building of houses in the suburbs; they also stimulated nonresidential construction in suburban areas. In 1954 Congress enacted a change in the tax law enabling developers to exploit the construction of new properties as a tax shelter. Under a complex arrangement, the depreciation costs of a commercial structure could be written off in the early year of its life. In other words, developers could build a commercial property and use its depreciation cost to reduce the tax burden. By the mid-1960s this tax break was costing the Treasury $700 million per year as shopping centers, offices, and motels quickly mushroomed on green-field sites. Accelerated depreciation favored suburbia, since write-offs were greater for new construction than for renovation. The law did not allow depreciation of land on urban sites. These tax breaks also promoted apartment dwelling construction. Multifamily homes were only around 6 percent of total housing starts prior to the tax change. By the mid-1960s almost 50 percent were apartments. Some were in the central city, but many were in the suburbs. The tax law changes stimulated both nonresidential and apartment construction in the suburbs. By the late 1950s and early 1960s, suburbs were increasingly self-contained, with a mix of housing types as well as shopping and commercial facilities. By the 1970s suburbs were important entities in their own right as sites of commerce as well as places of residence.

There were other important infrastructural subsidies. In 1956 Congress passed legislation that gave grants for up to 55 percent of the cost of sewage treatment facilities. This aided all municipalities but particularly helped suburban communities to extend sewer lines deeper into the countryside. In 1972 the federal aid was increased to 75 percent of the cost, with an annual appropriation of $6 billion. Adequate sewage treatment, like roads and housing, was essential to large-scale suburban development.

By the 1960s there was a growing awareness that the growth of the suburbs was leading to the decline of the central cities. Initially, FHA worked against the minority and inner-city housing market and supported the racial segregation of suburbia. The policy changed in 1966, when more loans were made available for people in inner-city neighborhoods, but in the short term this only helped lower-income white flight to the suburbs. More recently, FHA has directed funds to the inner city. In 1976 tax breaks were offered for historic preservation to buildings and sites on the National Register of Historic Places. And in 1977 the Community Reinvestment Act made lending institutions release information on the locations of their loans to reveal any discrimination. So while federal policy was more sensitive to its suburban bias, it was too little, too late.

Suburbs were not just the result of federal government actions. Changes in technology also played a part. New forms of manufacturing production meant that single-story production plants had an advantage over the multi-story plants dominant in cities. Factories needed more land, and that was now available in the suburbs. The shift from train to truck as the primary mover of goods also freed factories from locations in the central city. As jobs spread out, so did the people, and as the population shifted toward the suburbs, so did retail establishments. Once set in motion, these power-ful centrifugal forces reinforced each other such that economic vitality and population both moved from the central cities toward the suburbs.

In many metropolitan areas race played a significant role. In selected inner-city neighborhoods, blacks moved into the housing market. The re-sultant white flight to the suburbs was reinforced by the integration of the school system. The racial shifting was most prevalent from 1960 to 1980 and involved white suburbanization and increasing proportions of minori-ties in certain central cities. In some cases the process was lubricated by property interests. Ed Orser (1994) tells the story of one community in Ed-mondson, in the Baltimore metro area, where "blockbusting techniques" of scare tactics were used to encourage white owners to sell cheap, followed by high markups for black buyers who lacked access to conventional bank mortgages. There was a dramatic shift in the area's population between 1955 and 1965 as whites moved out and blacks moved in. White flight was an important part of the suburbanization of Megalopolis.

The fiscal needs of local municipalities also played a role in the creation of the liquid city. Given the municipal balkanization of the U.S. metropolis, each separate municipality needs to maximize its tax base. Municipalities compete for tax revenue-generating developments such as housing, offices, factories, and retail establishments. Instead of metropolitan-wide planning to ensure an orderly context for growth, there was a municipal scramble for development; it was a zero-sum game as one municipality's gain was perceived as another's loss. Municipalities were eager, and in some cases desperate, to attract development projects. The consequence was a wide suburban spread of developments.

Federal subsidies for roads, owner occupation, and greenfield commer-cial developments plus municipal encouragement for new developments all made the suburbs an attractive place for the private market. House builders and real estate developers all found greater encouragement and resultant profit in the suburbs. Private investment shifted toward suburban districts. Growth attracted more growth. New housing lured new commercial de-velopments, such as out-of-town shopping centers that in turn brought in more suburban development. There was an upward cycle of suburban growth leading to more suburban growth. Meanwhile, in another part of the metropolitan universe, the central areas of many cities were becoming underfunded and undercapitalized.

POPULATION REDISTRIBUTION WITHIN MEGALOPOLIS

The lubrication of suburbanization in Megalopolis was successful. In 1950 the population of Megalopolis was concentrated in the urban cores: more than 1 in 5 of the total population lived in the five large cities of Baltimore, Boston, New York, Philadelphia, and Washington. By 2000 fewer than 1 in 10 lived in these same areas. Whereas the central cities once dominated Megalopolis, by 2000 much of the population and vitality of the region had shifted to the suburban counties. The region changed from a big-city population to a much more fully suburbanized agglomeration.

I calculated the population residing in both central cities and surrounding suburban counties of each metropolitan statistical area and primary metropolitan statistical area in the region for both 1950 and 2000. The results, shown in Table 3-2, indicate substantial suburbanization. In 1950 one in two residents of Megalopolis lived in a central city and fewer than one in five lived in a suburb. By 2000, two out of three lived people in the suburbs. The urban cores had almost zero population increase in the 50-year period while the suburbs grew by almost 400 percent. One important countervailing trend is the continuing concentration of population in New York City. Unlike many other central cities in the United States, New York increased its population slightly from 1950 to 2000, from 7.89 million to just over 8 million. A more typical city trajectory is Baltimore City, which in 1950 had a population of almost 1 million. By 2000 this had fallen to 651,154. The surrounding county, Baltimore County, in contrast, increased its population over the same period, from 270,273 to 744,292. While the urban core lost almost a third of its population, the encircling suburban county gained more than 179 percent.

How does the population redistribution in Megalopolis compare with national trends? In 1950 only 23 percent of the U.S. population was living in the suburbs of metropolitan areas, but by 2000 this figure had increased to 50 percent. The suburbanization of metropolitan populations is the largest single population shift in the United States in the second half of the 20th century. In 2000 one in two Americans lived in suburban areas of

Table 3-2.   Population Redistribution in Megalopolis

	1950	2000
Population of central cities	16,435,953	16,453,210
Percentage of Megalopolis population	51.4	33.7
Population of suburban counties	6,284,393	31,228,502
Percentage of Megalopolis population	19.6	64.0

metro regions. In Megalopolis it was two out of every three. Megalopolis has a much higher level of suburbanization than the national average.

The extension of the urban region beyond the dense central cores creates a thinner spread of population across a wider area. This form of urban development, often termed urban sprawl, embraces the suburban strip, the highway system, and the automobile. Linear rather than nucleated developments are the rule, and the emphasis is on mobility and movement rather than stability and community.

Suburbanization also has political effects. Large, dense cities are sites of heterogeneous populations that need to have political discourse with one another to make local politics work. As more people move to suburban municipalities and school districts, they leave behind a political space shared by different racial and ethnic groups to live in more homogeneous suburban districts and municipalities. Local political spaces within Megalopolis are more homogeneous as more people live in residential areas surrounded by people who look like them. Suburbanization promotes a political monotone to the discourse of local politics and increases fiscal disparities between central city and suburban municipalities.

DECLINE AND GROWTH

There has been a dramatic population redistribution within Megalopolis. The areas of most marked population decline have been the central cities, especially Baltimore, Boston, Philadelphia, and Washington (Table 3-3). Over the past 50 years there has been a relative decline in the population of these large urban cores. In 1950 more than 4.6 million people, 14 percent of the total population of Megalopolis, lived in these cities. By 2000 this figure had fallen to 3.3 million, or 6.8 percent. This decline has significant implications for the viability of city governments. The loss of population signifies reduction in the tax base, a loss of revenue, and a decline in economic vitality. The population figures represent a radical change of met-

Table 3-3.   Areas of Population Loss in Megalopolis

	Population		
	1950	*2000*	*Percentage change*
Baltimore	949,708	651,154	-31
Boston	801,444	589,141	-26
Philadelphia	2,071,605	1,517,550	-27
Washington	802,178	572,059	-29

ropolitan fortunes, and the politics of growth and growth management in rapidly expanding suburbia contrast with the politics of decline and decline management in shrinking central cities.

Areas of decline were also noted in some of the more peripheral areas such as Lackawanna, Pennsylvania, and Berkshire, Massachusetts. Too far for large-scale commuting to major cities and without dynamic economic growth, these areas saw a loss of population.

Within the broader regional context of increasing population size, hot spots of remarkable increase were in newer suburban areas, such as Fairfax and Prince William counties in Virginia, Ocean County in New Jersey, and Howard County in Maryland (Table 3-4).

Growth in the southern part of the region has been significant. Around Washington and in the Washington-Baltimore corridor, an influx of jobs and people transformed previously rural areas. Howard County in Maryland, for example, had a population of only 23,119 in 1950. It was a rural area dominated by agricultural land use. Growth took the form of a private-sector "New Town," named Columbia, with very stringent planning controls, built by the Rouse Corporation. By 2000 the population of the county was 247,842, an increase of almost 1,000 percent. In northern Virginia growth was more piecemeal: in Loudoun County, for example, development occurred in a less orderly way as the population soared from 21,147 in 1950 to 169,599 in 2000.

This growth in southern Megalopolis reflects the rise of Washington as an important urban center. It is the urban manifestation of the growth of the military-industrial-scientific-security complex that has generated jobs and population growth. In 1950 the Washington metro area was relatively small. Since then we have witnessed the rise of "imperial" Washington, the capital of today's only global hyperpower, with attendant economic activities of government procurement contracts and the creation and growth of public and private research establishments, such as the National Institutes of Health in Bethesda, Maryland.

Table 3-4.   Areas of Population Growth in Megalopolis

County	Population		
	1950	*2000*	*Percentage change*
Prince William, VA	22,612	280,812	1,142
Howard, MD	23,119	247,842	972
Fairfax, VA	98,557	969,749	884
Ocean, NJ	56,622	510,916	802
Loudoun, VA	21,147	169,599	702

SUBURBAN DIVERSITY

Although we have made a distinction between declining central cities and expanding suburbs, it is important to note that the traditional city-suburb divide no longer suffices as a standard measure of comparison. Hanlon et al. (2006) are the latest commentators to show that the new metropolitan reality is heterogeneous suburbs. In their study of metro areas in the United States, they found pockets of poverty and decline, dispelling the myth of suburban uniformity. Lucy and Philips's (2000) examination of 554 suburbs in 24 states found that, from the 1960s to the 1990s, 20 percent of suburbs declined faster in median family incomes than their central cities. Chapter 7 will look at differences between suburban counties, and Chapter 8 will examine differences within suburbs in more detail.

Puentes and Warren (2006) identify what they call "first suburbs," defined as counties that were metropolitan counties adjacent to a metro core in 1950. As the development of these suburbs occurred over both time and space simultaneously, we will use the term *first* and *inner ring* interchangeably; *first* refers to their temporal development in the metropolis, and *inner ring* references their spatial configuration. The authors identify 64 first suburban counties with a total population of 52.3 million people in 2000, or approximately 18.6 percent of the national population. Of these 64 first suburbs, 28 of them were in Megalopolis, comprising a total population of 16.7 million people (Table 3-5). More than a third of the population of this region lives in the first suburbs. Table 3-6 shows how the population of Megalopolis is now distributed among central cities, first suburbs, and

Table 3-5.   First Suburbs in Megalopolis, 2000

Arlington, VA	Lehigh, PA
Baltimore County, MD	Middlesex, MA
Bergen, NJ	Middlesex, NJ
Berks, PA	Montgomery, MD
Bucks, PA	Montgomery, PA
Burlington, NJ	Nassau, NY
Camden, NJ	New Haven, CT
Delaware, PA	Norfolk, MA
Essex, NJ	Northampton, PA
Fairfield, CT	Prince George's, MD
Hampden, MA	Providence, RI
Hartford County, CT	Union, NJ
Hudson, NJ	Westchester, NY
Lackawanna, PA	Worcester, MA

Source: Based on Puentes and Warren 2006.

Table 3-6.   Population Distribution in Megalopolis

2000 Population (million)	Percentage of Megalopolis
Central cities 16.4	33.5
First suburbs 16.7	35.5
Newer suburbs 15.1	31.0

newer suburbs. Because Megalopolis is one of the older urban regions, not surprisingly the inner-ring suburban counties have the largest percentage of its population. Megalopolis is an urban region with a concentration of inner-ring suburbs.

Puentes and Warren (2006) point out first suburbs that evolve from fast-developing to moderately growing areas and undergo rapid racial and ethnic change, with an aging population. There are some first suburban counties in Megalopolis that easily fit this category; however, within Megalopolis there are significant differences between first suburbs in the northern and central parts of the region, in Connecticut, Massachusetts, New Jersey, and New York, and the faster-growing counties around Washington in Virginia and Maryland. While Worcester, Massachusetts, saw only a 5.8 percent increase in population from 1990 to 2000, Montgomery County, Maryland, experienced a growth rate of 14.5 percent. The different rates relate to the more recent nature of extensive growth in the southern first suburban counties compared with more fully built-out central and northern counties. Table 3-7 summarizes this trend with a sample of two inner-ring suburbs in different parts of Megalopolis, one in New Jersey and one in Maryland. Both Middlesex County, New Jersey, and Montgomery County, Maryland, are inner-ring suburbs, but they have different growth trajectories. Middlesex had a larger absolute population in 1950, indicative of an already-mature suburban county, and its growth rates were always less than Montgomery's. The difference was so marked that by 2005 Montgomery had a larger total population than Middlesex. Loudoun County is included in the table as an example of a newer suburban county in the Washington area. Notice how the growth rates took off in 1970, accelerating again from 1990.

Table 3-7.   Growth Rates in Inner-ring and Newer Suburbs

	Population	Percentage change			Population
	1950	1950-1970	1970-1990	1990-2005	2005
		Inner-ring suburbs			
Middlesex, NJ	264,872	120.4	14.9	17.6	789,516
Montgomery, MD	164,401	218.0	44.7	22.5	927,583
		Newer suburbs			
Loudoun, VA	21,147	75.6	131.8	196.6	255,518

The data tell two stories: first, of the general spread of the population, first into the inner ring of suburbs from 1950 to 1970, and second, of movement into the newer suburbs after 1970 and especially since 1990. Grafting onto this general Megalopolis-wide pattern are regional differences, with the inner-ring suburbs around Washington growing more rapidly.

Counties are coarse grids to identify the patterns of first suburban decline mentioned by Puentes and Warren. Decline is most easily discernible at the census place level (Hudnut 2003, 2003; Orfield 2002). Hanlon and Vicino (2005) in their analysis of inner-ring suburbs around Baltimore at the census place level were able to pinpoint areas of little or no population growth, increasing poverty rates, and declining property values. Decline was most evident in suburbs that had witnessed loss of manufacturing employment.

In the most problematic first suburban areas of Megalopolis, some housing stock is no longer marketable, infrastructure is in need of repair, and residents are dying off without a younger generation to replace them. Many of these suburbs experience economic and social problems normally associated with central cities, such as rising crime rates and poor schools.

The extent of the centrifugal movement of population is now beginning to cause problems for an inner ring of suburbs that have an obsolescent housing stock and an aging population.

A RETURN TO THE CITY

Although the 50-year data range shows decline in central cities, when we break it down by decade, a more varied pattern emerges. Since 1990 and in some cases 1980 there has been a small but significant rebound in certain cities. Between 1990 and 2000, central areas in New York, such as the Bronx and Queens, increased their populations by 10.7 percent and 14.2, respectively, with absolute increases of 128,861 and 277,781. This trend reverses decades of population loss. Another example is Boston. In 1950 the city had a population of 801,444. The population declined each census until 1980, when it bottomed out at 562,994. Thereafter the population increased, to 574,283 in 1990 and to 589,141 in 2000. The halt of the decline reflects the ending of the war on the city that was urban renewal. The demolitions had halted by the 1980s. When we look in closer detail, we see that the majority of Boston's growth was in two areas, Dorchester and East Boston, which experienced an influx of foreign immigrants. Just over 31 percent of Dorchester's population and 41 percent of East Boston's population was born overseas.

Not all central cities experienced rebound. In Philadelphia the population declined from 1,585,577 in 1990 to 1,517,550 in 2000 and declined even further to 1,414,245 in 2004. Baltimore's population declined from 736,014 in 1990 to 651,154 in 2000 and slipped to 609,779 by 2004. And in both cities the remaining population was proportionately more poor and black.

What is happening? Certain cities, such as New York and Boston, unlike Baltimore and Philadelphia, are experiencing a slight population rebound because the local economy is buoyant enough to generate employment growth. The population returning to the central city consists of two main types; single persons or professional households without children, and foreign-born immigrants. For both groups the return is fueled by employment and housing opportunities not available in the suburbs.

A 50-year period provides a long-term view of population growth and decline. Looking at more recent changes allows a finer-grained view. Between 1990 and 2000 Megalopolis had a population increase of 7.9 percent, which made it one of the slower-growing regions of the country, compared with states in the South and West. There were substantial variations within the region. Economically depressed areas, such as Baltimore, Philadelphia, and industrial counties in Pennsylvania and New England, showed the largest declines. Baltimore City lost 12 percent of its population from 1990 to 2000, while Philadelphia lost 4.3 percent and Lackawanna, Pennsylvania, lost 2.6 percent.

A TALE OF TWO PLACES

At either end of the continuum of population growth and decline in Megalopolis are Loudoun County in Virginia and Baltimore City in Maryland (Table 3-8). In 1950 the population of Loudoun County was only 21,147. By 2000 it reached 169,599, and in 2004 it rose to 239,156. Since 1950 the population has increased 1,130 percent; it increased by 41 percent just from 2000 to 2004, when Loudoun County was the fastest-growing county in the state. Situated close to Washington, the county has seen spectacular growth. The blistering rates reflect the booming government-related job market and the consequent generation of associated retail and service employment. The county is a magnet for newcomers and from 2000 to 2004

Table 3-8.   A Tale of Two Places: Baltimore City, MD, and Loudoun County, VA

	Baltimore	Loudoun
Population 2004	636,251	239,156
Population change 1950–2000	–31%	70.2%
Population change 1990–2000	–11.55%	96.8%
Population change 2000–2004	–2.3%	41.0%
Median household income	$30,078	$80,648
Median value of owner-occupied units	$69,100	$200,500
Percentage of population +25 with bachelor's degree	19.1	47.2
Percentage foreign-born	4.6	11.3
Percentage white	31.0	79.6

attracted one in four of all newcomers to the Washington metro area. It is the fastest-growing metro area outside of the Sunbelt. Almost 50 people move to the county every day, and 3,500 additional children enroll in the public schools each year. All this growth has its proponents eager to see further development, as well as its detractors, who draw attention to the costs of growth.

The rate of growth is rapid enough to cause such high levels of traffic congestion and pressure on local schools and services that a slow-growth backlash has emerged. In 1999 eight county supervisors were elected on a slow-growth platform, and the newly elected board of supervisors consequently cut the number of new houses planned for the county by 80,000. A response to this was seen in the 2003 elections. Developers gave $460,000 in campaign contributions to progrowth candidates, funded 200 legal challenges to the growth regulations, and helped found a prodevelopment group called Citizens for Property Rights. The new, progrowth board elected in 2003 soon created a plan for the county that overturned the previous slow-growth approach, withdrew authority to collect fees from developers to offset school construction, revised plans to build new housing, rescheduled historic preservation plans, extended water and sewer lines to aid further development, and created fast tracks for businesses seeking county approval. In 2005 the Virginia Supreme Court dismissed Loudoun's more stringent growth controls, effectively opening the less developed western part of the county to developments that may bring some 58,000 houses.

The new suburbanites and their experience with growth congestion have affected the wider political landscape. In the November 2005 Virginia gubernatorial election, Democratic candidate Timothy Kaine, campaigning on a restricted growth policy, beat the Republican in this traditionally Republican state. Although the Republican candidate won rural Virginia, the

Democrat won in the Megalopolitan counties of northern Virginia, including Loudoun. Kaine successfully pushed the message of restricted growth to suburbanites. In Loudoun County, which voted 53 percent to 46 percent for George W. Bush over John Kerry in the 2004 election, Kaine defeated the Republican by 52 percent to 46 percent. Soon after his election victory, in early December 2005, Kaine promised at a meeting in Loudoun that he would craft legislation that would allow localities to turn down housing construction proposals if transportation networks were deemed insufficient to support the increased population. In their detailed analysis of the election, Lang and Dhavale (2005b) show how Kaine's win was based on his success in this part of the state and the crafting of a message to appeal to outer suburban voters in a fast-growth region.

The experience of Baltimore City is in deep contrast. In 1950 the city had a population of almost one million. By 2004 the number of residents had fallen to only 636,251. The decline has been steady. From 1990 to 2000 the city lost 11.5 percent of its population, and from 2000 to 2004, a further 2.3 percent. Behind this population decline is the steady loss of the white middle class and, more recently, the black middle class as the city turns into a predominantly poor, black city, with few foreign-born immigrants and a poorly educated workforce. Yet the decline is not total. Neighborhoods such as Federal Hill have seen a restoration in the housing stock and the influx of professionals. Against a background of selective gentrification, however, the city has high levels of vacant housing. The population loss has reduced much of the tax base as well as the vitality of many city communities. Away from the high-profile "success" of Inner Harbor, Baltimore is a city in decline. The decline has prompted all manner of redevelopment schemes, including the Camden Yards baseball stadium, a new football stadium, and a convention center. But the steady hemorrhaging of population undermines even the best plans.

Baltimore and Loudoun: two ends of the population change continuum of Megalopolis—the declining central city and the exploding suburban county. Their fates are of course linked. Center cities' loss is the suburbs' gain as the population redistributes. There are countervailing tendencies in each place. In Baltimore, population loss depresses housing demand and real estate prices. There are now people moving out from the higher-priced Washington housing market to Baltimore, where comparable housing is much cheaper. Complex and long commutes to work are the trade-off for affordable housing. And in Loudoun County the experience of unplanned and rapid growth is creating demands for a restricted growth policy. The differing experiences of these two places reflect the primary forces shaping

Megalopolis, as population ebbs from certain cities and flows to selected suburban counties.

THE POPULATION OF MEGALOPOLIS

The basic population distribution data are interesting but limited: they allow us to answer only the question of where people are. But we are also interested in who is where. In later chapters we will use finer-grained analysis, but for the moment it is interesting to note, even at the coarse level of county data, who is where. Households differ in income, education, ethnicity, and family structure. I will consider some of the diagnostic variables of these dimensions that allow us to see how the population of Megalopolis compares with the rest of the U.S. population and also to note the differences across the region. Again the reader is directed to the data displays in the electronic atlas of Megalopolis at http://www.umbc.edu/ges/student_projects/digital_atlas/instructions.htm.

Almost one in every four people aged 25 and over in the United States has a bachelor's degree. Megalopolis has one of the higher figures in the country, at 28.4 percent; that compares favorably with other areas of high educational attainment, such as Colorado at 32.7 percent and Washington State with 27.7 percent. Megalopolis far outperforms Arkansas and Mississippi, where only 16.7 percent and 16.9 percent, respectively, of the residents are college graduates.

The Washington metro area represents one of the peaks of educational attainment in the region. The highest figure, 60.2 percent, is found in Arlington, Virginia. Montgomery County, Maryland, has many workers in government and scientific fields; the National Institutes of Health and associated biotech companies are located here. Nearby Howard County is home to educated workers in the white-collar local economy as well as government and private companies in Washington and Baltimore. In Montgomery and Howard counties, slightly more than 50 percent of the people over 25 have at least a bachelor's degree. Other areas of high educational attainment include New York and selected suburban counties surrounding New York City and Boston. Somerset, New Jersey, has 46.5 percent; while Middlesex, Massachusetts, has 43.6 percent. These cities and selected surrounding counties are home to those involved in the manipulation and interpretation of data and ideas that require education beyond high school diplomas. Relatively low levels of educational attainment are located in the declining industrial areas and more peripheral rural areas, such as Carbon, Pennsylvania (11 percent), Caroline, Maryland (12.1 percent), and Salem, New Jersey (15.2 percent).

Education and income are related; the higher the educational attainment, on average, the greater the income. The median income in 1997 across the region was $46,684, making Megalopolis one the more affluent parts of the United States. A belt of affluence stretches through the suburban counties from southern Virginia through Maryland and New Jersey up to New York and into New England. Counties within this belt include Fairfax, Virginia ($71,057), Howard County, Maryland ($68,024), Somerset, New Jersey ($74,586), Rockland, New York ($58,362), Fairfield, Connecticut ($56,872), and Norfolk, Massachusetts ($54,528), and all have median household incomes well above the regional and national figures. Within this suburban band of affluence are pockets of relative poverty in central cities: Baltimore ($27,713), Philadelphia ($28,897), and the Bronx ($24,031). Lower median incomes are also found in the declining industrial regions of Pennsylvania and New England, where counties such as Lackawanna, Pennsylvania ($32,536), and Providence, Massachusetts ($34,311), have household income levels below the regional and national levels. Surrounding the belt of affluence are the more rural peripheral counties of the region, such as Caroline, Maryland ($32,902), and Perry, Pennsylvania ($39,305), which fall just either side of the national average. There is substantial variation in median income across Megalopolis and a resulting world of difference between, on the one hand, suburban affluence and, on the other, urban poverty and rural decline.

Almost 20 percent of the people under 18 years of age in the United States are below the poverty line. As a region, Megalopolis has fewer poor children, but there are substantial variations—from 3.9 percent in Hunterdon, New Jersey, to 41.9 percent in the Bronx. What stands out from the data is the high level of child poverty in the major urban areas: Washington, Baltimore, Philadelphia, New York, and Boston all rank as areas of concentrated child poverty, with at least 30 percent of the people under 18 below the poverty line. There is a marked inequality between central cities and suburbs. The former trap many children in poverty while the latter can act as a platform for later success. There is a fundamental cleavage between city and suburb that overlies race and class divisions to produce different life opportunities.

Households vary in size and composition. We can consider three variables that allow us to differentiate types of household formation: households with children under 18, female-headed households, and single-person households.

Almost one in every two households in the United States includes children under 18. Alaska and Utah, with 58.1 percent and 56 percent, respectively, stand out as states with a majority of such households. Megalopolis is slightly below the national average. Areas with many retirees, such as Barnstable, Massachusetts, and Cape May, New Jersey, and those with a larger proportion of elderly people, such as Lackawanna, Pennsylvania, and Talbot, Massachusetts, have figures lower than the national average. The central city areas of Washington, Baltimore, Philadelphia, New York, and Boston also have fewer households with children than the national average, in part a function of the selective suburbanization of nuclear families. Households with children are found in the suburbs whereas single-person households and childless households tend to be located in the central cities. Areas of more households with children than the national average include the recent growth counties around Washington, such as Stafford and Loudon, Virginia, as well as the family-dominated Bronx, which stands out as a central city area where 56 percent of households have children under 18. Apart from the Bronx, households with children are concentrated in suburban counties.

Significant changes have occurred in U.S. household structure in the past 30 years. There are more single-person households, more elderly households, and more households headed by a female. The typical husband-and-wife household is no longer so rigidly defined by cultural norms. Divorce, separation, and the greater economic independence of many women now lead to more female-headed households. A female now heads more than half of the households with children in the United States. Megalopolis has 56.6 percent compared with the national average of 58.6 percent, with a range from 69.7 percent in Androscoggin, Maine, to 38.9 percent in Nassau, New York.

Approximately one in four of all households in the United States consist of a single person. One-person households have been growing both absolutely and relatively in the past 30 years as typical family size and structure change and the nuclear family is no longer dominant. There are now more young single households than ever before. Megalopolis is close to the national average. There is a wide range in the region, from only 13.5 percent single-person households in Stafford County, Virginia, to 48 percent in New York City. In most of suburban Megalopolis, values are below the national average: most households have more than one person. Somerset, New Jersey, for example, has only 22.8 percent single-person households.

There is a central city bias for areas above the national mean, and clusters can be identified in Washington, Baltimore, Philadelphia, New York, and Boston. In Baltimore, Philadelphia, and Alexandria, Virginia, more than one in every three households are single-person. There are more housing opportunities for single-person households in the central city areas, and urban economies attract young singles.

Owner-occupation is now the dominant tenure type in the United States. Two-thirds of U.S. households are owner-occupied. Owners either own their homes outright or are paying a mortgage. Megalopolis is only slightly above the national mean, but there are dramatic differences within the region. The most obvious pattern is the relatively low figure in the main urban centers. In these areas private renting is an important tenure type, so the percentage of owner-occupied housing tends to fall—to 40.5 percent in Washington, 50 percent in Baltimore, 20 percent in New York, and 33 percent in Suffolk County, New York. In these inner-city areas there are poorer households unable to afford owner occupation as well as households that prefer to rent accommodations. The inner suburban areas, such as Essex, New Jersey (45 percent), and Prince George's County, Maryland (61 percent), also have less owner occupation than the national mean.

Higher levels of owner occupation are found in the suburban areas, such as Nassau County on Long Island, with 80 percent, where residential development is dominated by the construction of single-family, owner-occupied houses, and the more rural areas, such as Cumberland County, Pennsylvania (73 percent).

Households also vary by race and origin. We can consider two important variables, percentage African American and percentage foreign-born. We will look at these variables more closely in a later chapter, so for the moment we will only sketch in the broad picture.

African Americans constitute just over 12.3 percent of the entire U.S. population. The southern states, stretching from the Tidewater to the banks of the Mississippi, continue to have a higher than average African American population, a historic reminder of the slave populations that worked the tobacco farms and cotton plantations. In Megalopolis approximately 1 of every 10 persons classified themselves in the census as African American. Three areas of significant concentrations stand out: Baltimore, Washington, and Prince George's County, Maryland. Secondary areas of concentration occur in urban areas, including Philadelphia, New York, and Boston. African Americans in Megalopolis tend to be more urban than rural. This pattern reflects the destination for waves of African Americans who moved from the rural South to the urban North in search of economic opportunities and social freedoms. Higher than average figures are found along the central urban spine of the region from Washington to New York City, with much lower than average figures in the rural, more peripheral counties. New England, apart from the Boston area, has a lower than average representation of African Americans. In Megalopolis, as in the nation as a whole, there is a southern bias to the concentration of African Americans.

Just over 1 in 10 people in the United States and Megalopolis was born overseas. This figure has grown over the past 30 years as the increased immigration to the United States that began in the mid-1960s reached a peak in the 1990s. Within the region there is tremendous variation, from Queens, New York, with 46 percent foreign-born, almost 1 in every 2 people, to Perry County, Pennsylvania, with only 0.9 percent, or less than 1 in 100. The New York metro area, including Queens, Hudson, Kings, New York City, and the Bronx is the principal immigrant gateway in the region. In all five counties the foreign-born constitute more than 1 in 4 of the population. Secondary gateways can be identified in the Boston area and the counties on the western fringe of Washington, including Montgomery, Maryland, and Arlington and Fairfax, Virginia. The more rural peripheral counties in the region, including Cumberland, Pennsylvania, Merrimack, New Hampshire, and Androscoggin, Maine, have very low levels of foreign-born.

The foreign-born are a good indicator of economic growth: they are attracted to places where jobs and economic opportunities are more readily available, and once established, the immigrant groups attract other immigrant groups. Their clustering in the three metro areas of New York, Washington, and Boston is a function of better economic opportunities and the existence of expatriate communities that provide a platform for subsequent immigrants arriving in a new country.

In summary, the people of Megalopolis are better educated and have higher incomes than the rest of the country, but there are substantial variations within the regions. A belt of suburban affluence contrasts with peripheral counties of declining economic vitality and sites of big-city poverty. The region, like the nation, is heterogeneous, with marked differences in the people of the expanding and declining areas, the residents of the big city and the suburb. Even at the level of county data, the fragmentation of affluent and poor into different parts of the region is clear. The fluidity of the metropolis does not refer to the random mixing of the oceans, more to the canalized movement of an engineered water system.

SUMMARY FINDINGS

The empirical material in this chapter shows a number of basic trends:

- Megalopolis is the largest and densest urban region in the United States, with a 2000 population of almost 49 million.
- Megalopolis increased its absolute population but declined slightly in relative significance.
- There has been a marked suburbanization of the population; two of every three people now live in suburban counties.
- The inner-ring suburbs grew very quickly from 1950 to 1970, leveling off after 1990. Growth since 1990 is more directed at the newer suburban counties.
- Central cities' populations declined in absolute and relative terms. This has negative implications for the fiscal health of cities.
- One major exception to the general picture of central city decline is the continuing vitality of New York City.
- There is evidence of population rebound in selected central city areas, such as Boston and the Bronx and Queens in New York, fueled in large part by a more recent influx of foreign-born immigrants.
- The greatest area of growth was in the southern part of the region, especially in the suburban counties of Maryland around Washington and along the Washington-Baltimore corridor. This growth reflects the increasing economic importance of the federal growth machine.
- Megalopolis consists of a wide swath of suburban affluence contrasted with peripheral counties of declining economic vitality and sites of big-city poverty. There is early evidence of some decline in selected inner-ring suburban areas.

CHAPTER FOUR

ECONOMIC RESTRUCTURING

F luidity characterizes not just the population of the modern metropolis but also its economic structures. In the fast-changing world of consumer tastes, global shifts in manufacturing, and rapid worldwide investment flows, urban economies are neither solid nor constant. Marx and Engels referred to modern capitalism as a force that makes "all that is solid melt into air," and economist Joseph Schumpeter depicted it as a form of creative destruction. The instability is particularly evident in contemporary urban economies, where innovation and change are the only constants and corporate decisions unfold against the fluid background of globalization.

At the midpoint of the 20th century the economic dominance of Megalopolis seemed assured. Gottmann describes it as the hinge of the U.S. economy, the unrivalled center of the expanding U.S. economy with a quarter of all jobs in manufacturing. By 2000, major economic changes had occurred. In this chapter I will discuss six of the most important: the pressures on agricultural land, deindustrialization, growth of services, importance of government, changing nature of retail, and suburbanization of employment.

THE PRESSURES ON AGRICULTURAL LAND

It is perhaps strange to begin a chapter on economic activities in Mega-lopolis with a discussion of agriculture, but this age-old economic activity continues to exercise an influence even in this most urbanized part of the nation: 30 percent of its total acreage is devoted to agriculture. For one of the most urbanized regions of the country, this is still a relatively high figure and indicative of the persistence of agricultural practices in the midst of the most densely populated part of the nation.

Within Megalopolis the amount of land devoted to agriculture has a distinct pattern. At a regional scale, it reflects climatic conditions and the differential length of the growing season. The more northerly, colder coun-ties such as Hillsborough in New Hampshire have only 6.7 percent of land in agriculture, and more land is given over to forest cover. Agricultural land use increases as one moves south. Rural counties, such as Lancaster, Penn-sylvania, and Carroll and Queen Anne's, Maryland, have 64.8 percent, 55.6 percent, and 70.5 percent, respectively, of land in agriculture. In the more urban and suburban counties, less land is devoted to agriculture. The most urban areas such as the Bronx have no agriculture, and even suburban coun-ties have little: Suffolk County in eastern Long Island has only 6.1 percent of its land acreage in agriculture. Suburban sprawl is also spreading nonag-ricultural land uses across the landscape.

The extent of land devoted to agricultural production has been dwin-dling since 1950. As a case study we can consider the example of Maryland. Figures 4-1 and 4-2 show the percentage of land devoted to agriculture in Maryland in 1950 and 2001, respectively. In counties both near to and far from Baltimore and Washington, the same picture emerges: over the 50-year period there was significant loss of land devoted to agriculture. The overall figure for the state was a decline from 65 percent of land in agriculture in 1950 to only 34 percent in 2001. Table 4-1 tells a similar story of declining amounts of agricultural land in four counties widely spread throughout the region. I have considered the period 1974 to 2002 because the Census Bu-reau's definition of "farm" remained constant during this time: "any place from which $1,000 or more of agricultural products were produced and sold, or normally would have been sold, during the census year." In two of the counties, the number of farms declined. The increase in Loudoun and Cumberland is, in part, due to the growth of hobby farms, but in the more traditionally rural counties the number of farms has declined.

Attempts to preserve agricultural land have been made throughout the region. One of the most successful schemes is in one of the more populous

Table 4-1.   Farms in Four Megalopolis Counties, 1974 and 2002

	1974	2002
Cumberland, ME		
Farms	398	596
Average size (acres)	160	91
Percentage land in farms	11.3	9.7
Loudoun, VA		
Farms	714	1,516
Average size (acres)	310	109
Percentage land in farms	66.8	49.7
Orange, NY		
Farms	891	706
Average size (acres)	170	153
Percentage land in farms	29	21
Wyoming, PA		
Farms	418	358
Average size (acres)	203	173
Percentage land in farms	33.2	24.2

Source: Agricultural census.

and affluent counties in Maryland, Montgomery County, situated just north of Washington. Economic growth and population increase have long placed heavy development pressures on the county. In 1964, the county adopted a planning policy called Wedges and Corridors to concentrate development along transportation corridors, with wedges of preserved open space to separate the developed areas. However, development pressure continued to pick up pace as the Washington metro area continued its economic growth, and between 1973 and 1979, Montgomery County lost 12,268 acres of farmland. A new master plan adopted by the county council in 1980 limited development to one dwelling per 25 acres in an area designated as the Agricultural Reserve—approximately 93,000 acres of the county's remaining contiguous farmland and rural open spaces. The reserve constitutes almost a third of the county's land surface. To compensate farmers and landowners, a transferable development rights (TDR) system was also introduced.

Under the TDR system, landowners retain "development rights" to one dwelling per five acres that can be used elsewhere in the county, called receiving areas. Landowners can sell the excess development rights to developers interested in building at densities higher than otherwise allowed in other parts of Montgomery County. The county planning board and council designate receiving areas that are located where schools, roads, and utilities are already in place or along major transportation corridors. Farmers, who are very often land rich and cash poor, can realize some liquid capital

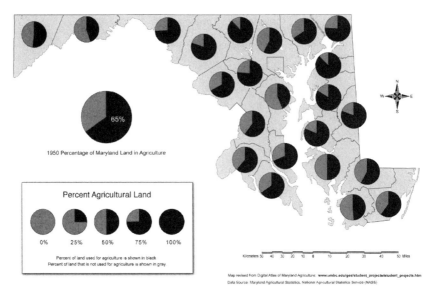

Figure 4-1.   Agricultural Land Use in Maryland, 1950

from the value of their land while still retaining farming use under the TDR system.

From 1971 to 1980, before creation of the TDR program, an average of 2,700 acres was subdivided annually in the Agricultural Reserve. Between 1981 and 1998, the figure declined to 460 acres per year. Compare this with Loudoun County, on the Virginia side of the Washington metro area, which also experienced heavy development pressure but had much fewer land-use controls. Loudoun lost more than 20,000 acres of farmland in only 10 years, between 1987 and 1997. By the time of the economic census in 1997, the Agricultural Reserve in Montgomery comprised 546 farms with a market value of $28.5 million and provided as an additional benefit an agricultural landscape of serene beauty in an area dominated by suburban sprawl. The policy was a success. Montgomery County has managed to preserve almost 90,000 acres from nonfarm development and kept land in agricultural production through county and state conservation easement programs that allow farmers to limit voluntarily development on their property. The county's farmland preservation programs are run by the Agricultural Services Division of the Department of Economic Development. This division oversees traditional agricultural economic assistance, such as drought relief, as well as the county's conservation easement programs. The department's staff members are familiar figures in the farming community.

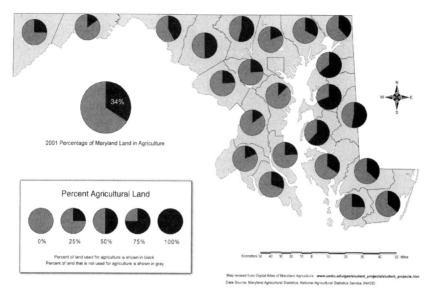

Figure 4-2.   Agricultural Land Use in Maryland, 2001

They often act as advocates for farmers when dealing with other agencies. As a result, many farmers have come to trust the agency.

Development pressures continue, often in new forms. The initial plans for the Agricultural Reserve did not include federally tax-exempted institutions, such as schools and churches. However, even these institutions constitute a strong development pressure. Conflict came to a head in plans for a 2,000-member megachurch on a 120-acre site. The plan was quashed in November 2005 when the county council withdrew the exemptions. The Agricultural Reserve is not a fully protected reserve that is immune to challenge; rather it is a shield under constant assault in various forms. Yet the lesson from Montgomery County is that preserving agricultural land is feasible even in areas facing severe development pressure.

Despite the decline in agricultural land area, crop yield data show an interesting spatial distribution in terms of prices, which range from just over $50,000 per acre of cropland in Richmond County, New York, close to New York City, to less than $25 in Warren County, Virginia. The very largest figures cluster around New York City, and consistently high figures are found along the coastal spine from Delaware through Massachusetts. At first blush, the data seem counterintuitive: the highest yields are found in the most urbanized counties outside of the central cities. We associate farming with distance from the cities, not with proximity. But the figures measure dollar yield per acre and are thus an indication of farming intensity.

A model of such intensity around the city was first developed as far back as 1826 by a German landowner, Johan Heinrich von Thunen (1783–1850). Von Thunen noted a pattern to land use and postulated a general model of land use around a city situated on a flat plain with homogeneous fertility and transportation costs. Farmers' costs were based on the prices of land and transport. Since farmers paid lower transport costs closer to the city, land costs tended to be higher. Only farmers growing the more intensive crops, with high returns, could afford the land closer to the city. The net result was a concentric ring pattern with more intensive agriculture in closer proximity to the city.

Although the von Thunen model operates under the restricted condition of a flat plain with unvarying fertility, conditions that are rarely met in the real world, crop yields in Megalopolis do give empirical evidence of its validity. It is remarkable that a model developed in rural 19th-century Germany has relevance for the urbanized seaboard of the United States in the early 21st century. Land closer to the cities is much more expensive than land on the periphery of Megalopolis. If farmers do locate closer to the city, they need to engage in intensive high-yield farming, such as market gardens of fruits and vegetables. In some cases it is not so much distance as time of transportation that is important. Large cities require daily supplies of produce and other specialized agricultural products. Restaurants, for example, require daily supplies for their diners. Proximity to the city provides swift access but at the price of high land values, which in turn means that only intensive farming with high yields makes economic sense. Organic produce is another emerging market that yields a high dollar return per acre. Affluent consumers are willing to bear the greater costs associated with these products.

High-yield counties are located around New York City, Philadelphia, and Boston. There are other areas of relatively high yields, such as New Jersey, giving credence to the state motto, the Garden State, and Rhode Island and southern Connecticut. In part these high yields are a function of proximity to the cities as well as of soil fertility.

Land is being lost to agriculture as the suburban spread flows across the landscape, but the remaining farmland that is close to the city has become so expensive that very intensive forms of farming are required, including nurseries, greenhouse crops, and the production of higher-value, specialty products.

DEINDUSTRIALIZATION

Manufacturing has long played an important role in the life of the region as a significant employer and major source of revenue. In 1900 Megalopolis had almost one in two of all manufacturing workers in the entire country. By 1950 this number had fallen to one in three. The absolute numbers were still significant, and in 1954 there was an all-time high of 4.6 million manufacturing workers in Megalopolis, accounting for almost one-third of all nonfarm workers in the region.

Comparisons of economic data over time are difficult because of the classification system used by the economic census changes every five years. However, one category that has retained its consistency is that of production workers in manufacturing. I was able to compare their numbers for every county and metropolitan statistical area in the region from 1958 to 1997.

In 1958 Megalopolis had 3,154,916 production workers, making up 27 percent of the national total. By 1997, the numbers had fallen to 1,498,706, only 12.3 percent of the national total. There was a significant deindustrialization of the region in both absolute and relative terms. The region has lost more than 1.5 million manufacturing jobs since 1958, when one in four of all manufacturing production workers in the United States was in Megalopolis; by 1997 this figure had fallen to just over one in eight. The number of production workers in manufacturing has halved while the region's share of national manufacturing employment has shrunk. This region is no longer the manufacturing powerhouse of the U.S. economy now that manufacturing jobs across the nation have shrunk because of increased worker productivity and a greater proportion of spending is allocated to services rather than goods.

When we look more closely, we can see that the change is uneven over the region. Table 4-2 reveals patterns of marked decline in the manufacturing employment in the central cities and the effective suburbanization of manufacturing employment. Although the number of production workers

Table 4-2.   Manufacturing Employment in Megalopolis

	1958	1997
Production workers in central cities	1,553,394	451,484
Percentage	49.2	30.4
Production workers in suburbs	1,156,400	1,047,222
Percentage	36.6	70.5

Source: Economic Census.

in central cities fell from more than 1.5 million in 1958 to less than 0.5 million in 1997, the comparable figures for the suburban counties remained around 1 million. Manufacturing companies go in and out of business, and so the figures record the net effective change, which amounts to the deindustrialization of big-city Megalopolis and the continuing industrialization of the suburbs. The older, more unionized production centers were located in the central cities. The shift accompanies a move toward newer, and to an extent that varies by region, less unionized plants.

Consider the case of New York County, comprising all of Manhattan and a sliver of the Bronx. In 1958 it had one of the largest concentrations of manufacturing in the nation, with 335,369 production workers. By 1997 the figure had fallen to 93,784. The city declined dramatically as a manufacturing center. It was the same story for large cities across the region. Over the same time period, the number of manufacturing production workers in Philadelphia declined from 207,951 to 33,884, in Baltimore from 82,305 to 21,898, and in Boston from 63,845 to 12,521. The smaller, traditional manufacturing cities such as Waterbury, Connecticut, and Lowell and Worcester, Massachusetts, had declines of, respectively, 17,000 to 4,940, 13,045 to 3,540, and 25,548 to 8,780. Throughout urban Megalopolis there was a notable urban deindustrialization. If New York County, for example, had followed the national trend in manufacturing, jobs would have increased 3.6 percent rather than decreased 72 percent between 1958 and 1997. New York County and Megalopolis experienced a proportionately greater decline in manufacturing than the national average.

Areas of growth in manufacturing are scattered, but a distinct cluster appears in southern Maryland and northern Virginia. Growth rates in these areas are relatively large; Montgomery County in Maryland, for example, grew from 2,828 production jobs in 1950 to 7,196, and such jobs in Fairfax County in northern Virginia grew in the same time period from 507 to 7,658. However, the hemorrhaging of jobs from central city areas dwarfs these figures.

The loss of manufacturing jobs is not only a sectoral shift; it involves a major social change. Manufacturing jobs were relatively high-paying, highly unionized forms of work deeply rooted in images of certain forms of masculinity and closely linked with the character and feel of specific communities and neighborhoods. The loss of these jobs involved a major upheaval in the economic fortunes of these communities and in job opportunities for many unskilled and semiskilled males. Deindustrialization is a social process as much as an economic shift.

In 2000 in the United States 16.47 million people were employed both full time and part time in the manufacturing sector. Significant clusters are still found in traditionally industrial counties such as Middlesex, Massachusetts (118,002 manufacturing employees), New York (93,784), Hartford (71,982), Montgomery, Pennsylvania (67,234), Worcester, Massachusetts (61,344), and New Haven (59,380). Those places that rely heavily on manufacturing, such as Worcester, face an uncertain future as the sector continues to decline. Manufacturing-based local economies in Megalopolis must search for ways to diversify and expand the local economic base away from a shrinking sector.

THE GROWTH OF SERVICES

With the decline in manufacturing, there has been an increase in services, which now accounts for one in every three U.S. workers and almost 30 percent of the gross national product (GNP). "Services" covers a wide range, from jobs in health care and financial consultancy to computer information companies. The sector includes a range of wildly differing jobs. At one end are the high-earning Wall Street brokers working in finance and international currency dealing, receiving lucrative annual bonuses that fuel price increases in selected local housing markets. At the other end are contract cleaners of the offices that house these executives. One particularly dynamic sector of services is the knowledge-based industries or so-called producer services, such as banking, finance, business consulting, and information technology. Together these sectors constitute the dynamic edge of the U.S. capitalist economy. Since 1980 a local economy's success has rested less on manufacturing employment and more on the extent to which it can generate, retain, and attract knowledge-based industry. Financial services continue to be concentrated especially in the global cities, such as New York, where the economics of agglomeration and the importance of face-to-face contact continue to make big cities attractive places for business. Manhattan continues to resist deconcentration and loss of population in large part because of the vitality of advanced financial services in its downtown location. High-tech industries have aggregated around a number of innovation centers, such as Route 128 in Boston. Here the pull is other firms, links with local universities and government research labs, and the consequent pool of highly skilled labor.

As mentioned earlier, comparisons over time are made difficult by changes in classification. I have noted the number of workers in selected producer services from the most recently available data in the economic census of 1997 (Table 4-3). Although this is only a snapshot rather than a trend, what is truly remarkable is the extent to which Megalopolis remains a major center of selected producer services. Over 1 in every 2 workers in the nation in the important sector of finance and insurance is located in Megalopolis. And 1 in every 10 workers is based in the New York metro area. The figures are even higher for the subcategory of securities intermediation: 81 percent of all workers in the United States in this category are employed in Megalopolis, with 33 percent located in the New York metro area.

Although Megalopolis has shed many manufacturing jobs, it is home to information-processing sectors. Metro locations are still important for these producer services. The three sectors noted in Table 4-3 employed a total of 5,628,668 people in 1997, with 1,926,000, or 34.2 percent, in the four metro areas of New York (974,000), Washington (464,000), Philadelphia (266,000), and Boston (222,000).

The professional, scientific, and technical services sector is also important in Megalopolis. Almost 3 million workers are employed in this sector, well over half of all such workers in the entire country. The largest single centers are in Washington, with 285,204, and in New York City, with 249,161. In 1997 the two metro regions of New York and Washington-Baltimore had, respectively, 569,807 and 346,773 of these jobs, or 18 percent of the national total. Megalopolis is now more of an information-processing center than a metal-bashing economy. It is the analysis of information rather than the manipulation of metal that is now the defining economic characteristic and leading economic sector in Megalopolis.

THE IMPORTANCE OF GOVERNMENT

One important change in the national economic picture is the rise of government and the corresponding increase in the importance of the public sector to the operation of the private market. Two elements are important: the allocation of federal government funds and the growth of public employment.

The federal government is a major money machine, collecting taxes and spending revenues. Federal spending in 2001 totaled $1,863,900,000,000. This is a figure easier to read than to comprehend. The sheer magnitude of

Table 4-3.   Financial Services in Megalopolis, 1997

	Workers	Percentage of U.S. total
Finance and insurance	2,534,209	43
Securities intermediation	568,939	81
Information and data processing	113,665	33
Professional, scientific, and technical	2,980,794	57

Source: Economic Census.

U.S. government spending is staggering. Let me try to come to grips with it by considering different forms of federal spending.

According to the 2000 census, the national per capita spending of federal funds and grants was $5,562. The Megalopolis per capita figure is $6,902, well above the national average. Across the region there are substantial differences, from $52,088 per capita in Washington to $1,264 in Manassas Park, Virginia. The variation from the national average reflects two factors. First, a significant portion of this type of government spending is transfer payments to retired, disabled, and poor people through such things as housing assistance, food stamps, and Medicare. The cities—where there are more poor people—stand out as areas of increased federal spending, such as Baltimore City ($11,767 per capita) and Philadelphia ($8,865 per capita). Second, this form of government spending also includes compensation to federal workers as well as specific grants for such things as scientific research. This pattern of spending is particularly evident in the federal capital of Washington and surrounding areas. Arlington, Virginia, with $32,423 per capita and Alexandria, Virginia, with $20,233 per capita stand out as major recipients of federal dollars. The growth of the southern part of Megalopolis is based on high levels of federal employment and spending.

Government spending also takes the form of procurement contracts. The U.S. government requires a massive amount of goods and services. Government contracts are highly valued as they are always paid, backed as they are by the federal Treasury. The national average per capita for procurement awards in 1999 is $760. The figure for Megalopolis is $517, but the distribution of procurement contracts in Megalopolis is uneven, with the heaviest concentration around the Washington area. Companies and firms have located to this area to be close to the center of power and decision-making. The high per capita amounts in Washington ($11,194), Fairfax City ($79,138) and Falls Church ($48,616), Virginia, and Montgomery County ($4,041) and Prince George's County ($3,247), Maryland, are the main reason behind the growth of this region in the past 20 years. Each month *The Washington Post* publishes a list of contracts awarded in the technology sector. The following contracts are taken randomly from the issues of March

28 and December 5, 2005, a small sample of the drip feed of government procurement contracts into the local economy:

- Anteon of Fairfax, awarded a $117 million, five-year contract to support the U.S. Army's casualty care program in Iraq;
- Centurum of Arlington, awarded a $46.7 million, six-year contract for technical service support for the U.S. Navy's battlefield sensors;
- General Dynamics of Fairfax, awarded a $2.3 billion, five-year contract for information technology services to the U.S. Army;
- ITT of Alexandria, awarded a $57.3 million contract from Space and Missile Defense Command for lethality testing; and
- Radian of Alexandria, awarded a $4.3 million contract from the U.S. Navy for air-conditioners.

That brief sample is only a small glimpse of the tight nexus of the military-industrial-scientific complex that has grown up around Washington. Federal contracts are the basis for the spectacular economic growth of the Washington metro area. The largest economy in Megalopolis, the New York metro area, has a relatively low level of per capita procurement grants and awards. While the Washington metro area is dependent on the public sector, the New York metro area is more dominated by the private sector.

Government procurements, at the federal, state, and local levels, also lead the way in giving encouragement and preference to female-owned and minority-owned businesses. In the past 20 years these programs have enabled a more diverse group of people to benefit from government contracts. The creation of a female and minority entrepreneurial class has been aided enormously by preferential treatment in the awarding of government contracts.

Government spending influences private market decisions. The location of public highways, for example, has guided the form and level of private investment in suburban areas. The edge cities of out-of-town shopping malls and bedroom communities are as much creations of public spending as they are functions of private investment. Public investment provides an important container for private investment.

Government spending also plays a role in the location of fixed-asset investments, such as military bases and research centers. Across Megalopolis there is a wide scatter of military bases. In some cases the military base is a major employer in the local economy. Fort Belvoir is the largest single employer in Fairfax County in Virginia. The base employs 24,000 workers. Fort Meade in Anne Arundel County in Maryland generates 39,000 jobs, and Fort Monmouth is the third-largest employer in Monmouth County, New

Jersey. The plans announced by the Base Realignment and Closure Commission in May 2005 had important consequences for the local economies of Megalopolis. The largest absolute effects will be felt in the greater Washington metro area, with a projected net loss of 26,238 jobs with the closure of such bases as the Walter Reed Army Medical Hospital, and the growth of over 27,000 jobs in the suburban districts, including major expansions planned for Fort Meade (5,400 new jobs) and Fort Belvoir (18,000 new jobs). Although the absolute numbers were smaller elsewhere in the region, the relative effects were substantial. The planned loss of 8,457 jobs at the New London submarine base in Connecticut and the complete closing of Fort Munroe in New Jersey will have devastating effects on the local economies. Fort Munroe directly employs 5,272 civilian and military workers and indirectly supports 20,000 workers in the local region.

There are also civilian government institutions. One of the fastest-growing counties in Megalopolis is Montgomery County in Maryland. Its population grew from 164,401 in 1950 to 873,341 in 2000—a 431 percent increase while the increase for Megalopolis as a whole was only 53 percent. The county has a concentration of federal research laboratories and regulatory agencies that in turn attract high-technology companies, service industries, and vendors. Montgomery County is home to 19 major federal research and development and regulatory agencies, including the National Institute of Standards and Technology, National Institutes of Health, National Oceanic and Atmospheric Administration, Naval Medical Center, Nuclear Regulatory Commission, Food and Drug Administration, Department of Energy, Walter Reed Army Medical Center, U.S. Army Diamond Labs, and Consumer Products Safety Commission. The National Institutes of Health in Bethesda, for example, houses 12 research institutes employing 20,000 workers and has grants, contracts, and a procurement budget worth $9 billion. In the 1993 contract year, Montgomery County companies received 19 percent ($159.2 million) of the institutes' total U.S. research budget. The National Institute of Standards and Technology employs 2,600 scientists at its primary site at Gaithersburg, developing measurement standards for industry. The Food and Drug Administration, headquartered in Rockville, employs 4,500 people. A new $500 million consolidated campus for the agency is under construction at White Oak in Montgomery County. With this steady injection of federal dollars and the creation of secure and well-paid employment in the scientific research sector, it comes as no surprise that Montgomery County ranks as the ninth most affluent county in Megalopolis, with a median household income in 1997 of $62,130; the average for Megalopolis was $46,684, and for the nation, $37,005. More than half the people over 21 in the county have a bachelor's degree; the national figure is less than one-quarter.

Table 4-4 shows the top 10 counties (or municipalities) in terms of per capita federal spending in 2004. Four of them are in Megalopolis, clustered around the Washington metro area. Compared with the other places in the list, the Megalopolis counties have significant population, and thus receive vast amounts of money that ripple through the local economy. The heavy federal spending in this southern part of Megalopolis is an integral part of a complex economy, not an isolated case of a government establishment in the middle of nowhere. Federal spending constitutes an important part of the economic propensity and population increase of the southern rim of Megalopolis.

The public sector is an important employer in its own right. Immediately after World War II, the federal government's share of total employment fell almost to 9 percent. Since then it has remained around 10 percent with minor oscillations. In Megalopolis there is a substantial proportion of federal workers in the Washington metro area, where two of every three workers are employed by the federal government. Every county has at least some government employment. Dutchess County in New York is a typical example, with government employment constituting just less than 20 percent of total employment with the bulk of that in state and local government employment. The state bureaucracies in the state capitals—Boston; Harrisburg, Pennsylvania; Concord, New Hampshire; and Dover, Delaware—all boost the state and local government employment sector in their respective counties (Suffolk, Dauphin, Merrimack, and Kent).

Government employment, at least since the 1970s, has become more open to women and minorities. Data for state and local employment show

Table 4-4. Top Recipients of Federal Government Spending, 2004

	Per capita federal spending	Population
Falls Church, VA	*$145,164*	*10,781*
Fairfax City, VA	*$138,060*	*22,062*
Los Alamos, NM	$105,868	18,796
Arlington County, VA	*$52,254*	*186,117*
Anderson County, TN	$49,465	72,244
Sagadahoc County, ME	$38,922	36,927
Cheyenne County, CO	$37,947	2,030
Bristol Bay, AK	$35,188	1,103
King George County, VA	*$35,043*	*19,354*
Southeast Fairbanks, AK	$34,167	5,997

Note: Italics indicate counties in Megalopolis.

that, for 1999, 44.8 percent were women and 30.1 percent were minorities. Public employment has been a significant source of female employment and an important and vital platform for the creation of a black middle class.

Public employment is significant for city finances and urban politics. New York City alone employs almost half a million people with an annual payroll of $1.7 billion. Municipal employment is a major source of work and income in many of the larger and poorer cities of the nation. The increasing size of city payrolls is in part a function of rising demand for municipal services. However, it is not a simple case of municipal employment growing in line with rising needs. There is also pressure from public sector unions to win jobs and better conditions and mounting political claims from urban constituencies eager to benefit from municipal largesse. There is a long tradition in U.S. urban politics of ethnic constituencies coming into political power and sharing the spoils of political patronage. Municipal employment is part of the political compromise worked out by business elites and community leaders to maintain political peace and lubricate the smooth workings of urban regimes. Municipal employment is not just another job category; it is an important element in the ongoing struggle in the urban political arena.

THE CHANGING NATURE OF RETAIL

The suburbanization of retail was noted by Gottmann (1961) in his original study of Megalopolis. He described a shifting retail landscape of suburban shopping centers but failed to foresee their subsequent expansion. "In the suburbs," he wrote, "the people are too thinly spread to justify duplicating all the services of the central city with the frequency of the shopping centers. And to the suburban population, used to commuting, the better variety and quality of the services available in the central cities justify a trip to them" (*511*). Gottmann wrote these words at a time of downtown dominance, when shopping was still concentrated in the central city locations, and the big downtown department store was the flagship of the retail sector. In the past 50 years the flagship has turned into the Titanic.

Three trends have influenced the location of retail in Megalopolis. The first is the development of large suburban malls. In 1957 the Garden State Mall opened in Paramus, New Jersey. It was designed as a concentrated retail space with landscaped walkways, a large mix of stores, and lots of parking. It was removed from the parking constraints of the central city and located in cheaper suburban land. Before the mall opened, 70 percent of shoppers in the local suburbs shopped in New York City. Two years after the mall opened, only 50 percent shopped in New York City. The large department stores in New York City responded by opening branches in the mall. Today the Garden State Mall has 1.96 million square feet of retail space and 260 stores that include Macy's, Nordstrom, JC Penny, Neiman Marcus, and Lord and Taylor. Throughout Megalopolis major suburban shopping malls have become prime retail sites. These large malls have become anchors for subsequent suburbanization as people now do more of their shopping at suburban malls.

The second trend has been the growth of the strip as retail strung out along highways and roads. The big box retailers such as Wal-Mart, Target, Lowe's, and Best Buy look for cheaper suburban land close to good road connections. Retail has hemorrhaged from the downtown and bled all along radial strips around road and interstate connections.

The third trend is the decline of the downtown. There are some exceptions. New York City, for example, continues to have significant downtown shopping. And New York County still had 102,965 employees in retail, according to the 1997 economic census, although this was down from 224,853 in 1958. Elsewhere, the downtowns in large and small cities have shrunk in retail size and importance. The large department stores have closed in many cities, often leaving central cities underserved in terms of retail opportunities and providing yet another impetus for continued suburbanization. Although Baltimore City and Philadelphia have 5.7 and 3.3 retail workers per 100 population, the neighboring suburbs in Baltimore County and Montgomery County have 6.5 and 7.2, respectively.

The suburban shift in retail both led and followed the suburban shift in population. Initially, the suburban malls followed the suburbanizing population; later they helped attract further suburbanization. The spread of retail and the wider spread of population went hand in hand. Tysons Corner Mall, located 7 miles west of Washington, opened in 1968 and now houses just over 2 million square feet of retail space and 2,150 retail outlets with movie theaters, department stores, and specialty stores. In 2000 the Central Park Mall opened in Fredericksburg, Virginia; this 2.4 million-square-foot retail space is some 30 miles from Washington. The new mall's location both reflects and reinforces the southward spread of the Washington metro population.

Retail has shifted its center of gravity in the past 50 years from downtown to the suburbs, from central city department stores to suburban malls, and from city streets to suburban strips.

THE SUBURBANIZATION OF EMPLOYMENT

The net effect of the changes I have discussed is the suburbanization of employment. The popular notion of suburbanization is great expanses of subdivisions obliterating fields and farms. But another significant part of suburbanization has been the shift of employment from the city to the suburbs.

Joel Garreau (1991) identifies "edge cities" as centers with more than 5 million square feet of office space, 600,000 square feet of retail space, and more jobs than bedrooms situated on what was less than 30 years ago essentially a greenfield site or predominantly residential area. He finds 120 such edge cities around the country. It is interesting to note that most of them are located at the junction of interstate highways, reinforcing the point that the federal government has underwritten suburban expansion and edge city developments. According to Garreau, 37 of these 120 edge cities are in Megalopolis; they include 2 outside Baltimore (Towson and Hunt Valley), 5 in the Boston area (Kendall Square–MIT, Quincy-Braintree, Mass Turnpike–128, Burlington Mall, and Framingham), 16 outside New York City (Paramus-Montvale, Mahwah, Meadowlands, Whippany–Troy Hills, Bridgewater Mall, Woodbridge, Amtrak Metropark, Princeton, White Plains, Purchase-Rye, Great Neck, Mitchell Field–Garden City, Route 110–Melville, Hauppauge, Stanford-Greenwich, and Westport–I-95), 3 outside Philadelphia (King of Prussia, Willow Grove–Warminster, and Cherry Hill), and 11 in the Washington-Baltimore corridor (Bethesda, Silver Spring, I-270–Beltway, Rockville–I-270, Shady Grove–I-270, Gaithersburg-Germantown, Columbia, Rosslyn-Ballston, Crystal City, Old Town Alexandria, and Tysons Corner).

The edge city model has been subject to criticism. Robert Lang (2003a) suggests that Garreau overstates the case, and Megalopolis, with the exception of Washington, is now more of an edgeless region. With primary reference to rental office space, Lang suggests that, rather than new concentration at the edge of cities, the dominant form is freestanding buiidings, office parks, or small clusters of buildings at low densities dispersed along interstates and arterial routes. With low densities, an average of 20,000 square feet of office space per square mile, little mixed use, and limited access to mass transit, these commercial structures are not edge cities about to happen but very decentralized urban forms. In a follow-up study Lang et al. (2006) looked at office development in 13 cities and found that 40 percent of office space was in the form of edgeless cities. Within the four cities in Megalopolis that Lang et al. considered—New York, Boston, Philadelphia, and Washington—the respective figures were 32.3, 50.1, 54.3, and 24 percent. In New York, Boston, and Philadelphia the bulk of office space was either downtown or in edgeless cities, with New York still retaining a downtown dominance. Edge city development was very limited (Table 4-5). The one exception was Washington, where edge city development constitutes more than a third of the total regional office space. The polycentric nature of Washington, with three very large edge cities—Tysons Corner, Herndon-Reston, and Chantilly-Dulles—is the Megalopolis exception rather than the dominant form.

As Lang observes, edgeless cities represent the newest, "postpolycentric" phase in the continuing decentralization of the modern metropolis. Downtowns will continue to exist, especially for the information-intensive sectors such as publishing, financial services, advertising, banking, and law. New York, with a preponderance of these sectors, continues to have a dominant downtown. In Megalopolis only Washington fits the edge city description; elsewhere the urban form of edgeless cities dominates the geography of the suburban-oriented metropolis.

Jobs have proven more fluid than some of the lower-income urban population. While employment opportunities have suburbanized outward, some low-income, particularly minority, populations have been effectively trapped in the inner city. A combination of discrimination and poverty has restricted housing choices for some of the poorest citizens. They have seen jobs shift to more distant and less accessible suburban locations while they remain stuck in the city. This phenomenon has been referred to as spatial mismatch (see Brueckner and Zenou 2003; Kain 1993; Wilson 1996). The

Table 4-5.   Office Space in Four Cities of Megalopolis

	Total office space (million sq. ft.)	Percentage		
		Downtown	Edge city	Edgeless city
New York	222.052	61.4	6.3	32.3
Boston	101.776	43.3	6.7	50.1
Philadelphia	98.260	35.6	10.1	54.3
Washington	86.113	41.1	34.9	24.0

Source: Based on data in Lang et al. (2006).

nature of the mismatch is vivid in the case of Baltimore. In 1970 there were approximately 984,700 jobs in the Baltimore metropolitan area, and of these, 540,700, roughly 55 percent, were in the city. By 2000 there were 1,678,800 jobs in the metro area, but only 472,200, 28 percent, were in the city. Although the number of jobs in the metro region had increased, the city's share had fallen in absolute and relative terms. Poor people in the city have restricted mobility. Almost a third of households in the city do not have access to a private car, and a study by the Jacob France Institute of the University of Baltimore found that one-third of all low-skill job hires in the metro area in 1999 were inaccessible to the city's poor by mass transit and a further third were inaccessible by city bus routes (Stevens et al. 2001). Across Megalopolis a similar story unfolds of central city job loss and the effective suburbanization of employment and job opportunities. As jobs suburbanize, they spread out into a dispersed pattern unable to support public transport. Those without access to private cars, approximately one in three of all households in Baltimore, are effectively limited in their ability to obtain and hold down jobs.

THE LIQUID ECONOMY

Jobs have flowed from the urban centers toward the suburbs, and the movement is seemingly ceaseless. In October 2005 the governor of Virginia, Mark Warner, announced that CGI-AMES Inc. and Northrop Grumman Corporation would build a major technology center and hire close to a thousand people in Lebanon in Russell County, in southwestern Virginia, more than 200 miles from Washington and well outside even the most generous demarcation of Megalopolis. Both companies would rely on federal and state contracts, which are the vital elements in the military-scientific-technology complex that has fueled the Washington metro economy. Their decision to invest in this part of the state reflects a push away from the Megalopolis of traffic congestion, expensive housing, and skill shortages, as in Loudoun County. The companies will pay an average salary of $50,000, well above the $27,606 average salary in Lebanon but half what they would have to pay in Loudoun County. This small town of less than 3,500 people is in the middle of a depressed part of the state. The companies will be eligible for federal grants and state subsidies and will have access to state contracts. To compete for a $2 billion state technology contract, Northrop will invest in a $22 million technology center in Lebanon and hire 430 employees.

I draw two conclusions from the story of Lebanon, Virginia. The first is that companies are relentless in their pursuit of competitive edge. Technology companies set up initially in northern Virginia because of easy access to Washington, but as growth continues, labor costs increase—as do housing costs and traffic congestion—all adding a financial burden to individuals and companies. Greenfield sites in small towns farther away from Megalopolis offer the competitive advantage of cheaper labor and land costs. Just as jobs have flowed out from cites to the suburbs, they are now slipping as inexorably from congested suburban counties to more rural areas where land and labor are cheaper and government subsidies sweeten the deal.

The second conclusion I draw is that state and local government play vital roles in shaping corporate investment decisions and location strategies. The liquidity of employment opportunities and investment flows forces governments to compete to maintain and attract private investment. Subsidies, incentives, and tax holidays are all tactics used by state and local governments to make sure that the liquid economy does not flow away from or around them. The net effect is that state and local governments bargain away tax revenues in order to attract private investments. The liquidity of capital gives business a greater bargaining power than the literally fixed position of state and local governments. While government is stuck in place, the market flows on.

A TALE OF TWO COUNTIES

We can appreciate the range of megalopolitan economic structure by considering the differences between selected counties. Let us first consider a county at the region's margins, Lackawanna, in Pennsylvania. This county has seen population loss, 2.6 percent from 1990 to 2000 and 1.6 percent from 2000 to 2004. The population loss reflects the declining economic vitality of the area. It was not always so. In the 19th century the county was ideally poised to play a major role in the industrial revolution. The county lay atop a rich anthracite coal reserve and iron ore deposits. A canal was built to ship out the coal, and a nail-making factory, the first in the country, was completed in 1848. Coal and iron ore were the vital ingredients for the new metal-based manufacturing economy. The county was one of the hot spots of rapid growth in the 19th century, at the very frontier of the industrial revolution. The region attracted migrants from Western and Eastern Europe. The economy was buoyant. With the dawn of the 20th century the county began a long slow decline. Oil replaced coal as a major source of power, and the manufacturing plants began to close, as new plants were established in the Sunbelt and later in cheaper labor areas around the world. The economy shrunk and population decline set in. In 2003 the county had a population of 209,932, and of the 92,290 employees, 15.7 percent still worked in manufacturing, only 2.8 percent worked in information industries, and only 6 percent worked in the professional, scientific, and management industries.

Compare that with Loudoun County in Virginia. While Lackawanna was growing in the 19th century, Loudoun was a sleepy rural place. In the late 20th century, while Lackawanna saw shrinkage, Loudoun experienced spectacular growth, over 7 percent per annum since 1994. By 2004 its population was 229,429, making it one of the fastest-growing counties in the country. People were attracted to the jobs in the Washington metro area. Inside the county the largest single employer is America Online Inc., and of the 93,258 people in paid employment, 19.3 percent work in the professional, scientific, and management industry, 10.2 percent work in information, and only 6 percent work in manufacturing. The median household income in Lackawanna is $34,438; in Loudoun it is $80,648. Two counties, two very different experiences: Lackawanna and Loudoun, old economy and new economy, decline and growth, a downward spiral and an upward trajectory.

SUMMARY

In the past 50 years Megalopolis has undergone a profound economic transformation that includes a decline in the amount of land devoted to agriculture, a marked loss of manufacturing employment, the growth of services, the rise of government as a powerful economic motor, the suburbanization of retail, and the overall shift of jobs from cities to suburbs.

Areas of growth include the development of a military-industrial-scientific complex around Washington and the dynamic financial services sector in the New York metro area. Services have replaced manufacturing in the successful local economies. The leading economic sector in Megalopolis is the manipulation of information rather than the shaping of metal. Growth has taken place in the information economy, public services, and financial services.

A train journey from Washington to Boston on the main rail line gives a fascinating glimpse of the transformation of the economic landscape. The train passes by hundreds of abandoned and converted industrial factories as it follows the heart of the old industrial landscape of manufacturing; it is a journey that reveals the extent of decline and abandonment. Factories lie vacant, the machines long since stilled and the workers long since gone. The old factories that remain are boarded or converted, in some places to warehouses and in the more dynamic urban economies to condos and health clubs. The train ride is a journey through old industrial Megalopolis with an occasional sighting of the newer Megalopolis sprouting up away from the rail line along interstates and on prime suburban sites. The train travels across an urban landscape half-abandoned, shabby, dirty, aging gracelessly, with occasional glimpses of downtown renewal and expansion at the edges. One passes through an abandoned landscape and can see the new landscape emerging in the distance.

CHAPTER FIVE

IMMIGRATION

In 2005 Hugo Salinas announced his intention to run for mayor in the Salvadoran town of Intipuca. He did not make the announcement in El Salvador but in a hotel in downtown Washington, D.C. Streams of migration and remittances link the small town and the U.S. capital. More than 40 percent of the residents of the Salvadoran town now live in the Washington area, and they send money back to Intipuca and invest in its economy. Salinas, who lives in Arlington, Virginia, lost the election, held in March 2006, by fewer than 100 votes.

At the time that Gottmann was writing *Megalopolis*, the national percentage of the foreign born was around 6 percent, and immigration to the United States was limited. This era ended in the mid-1960s, replaced with a period of increasing levels of immigration from overseas. By 2000 the foreign-born proportion rose to 11.1 percent as almost 56 million people in the United States were either born outside or had at least one parent born outside the United States. In this chapter we explore the role of this increasing and widening stream of immigration to the demographic makeup of Megalopolis.

NATIONAL TRENDS

The span from 1950 to 2000, the focus of our attention, comprises two distinct immigration periods. The first, from 1950 to the mid-1960s, witnessed sluggish immigration. Previous immigrant groups, such as the Irish and the Italians, had prospered and, to an extent, Americanized as they moved out of the old neighborhoods and into the new suburbs. In this first period, then, with the lifeblood of new immigration closed off and the economy booming, white ethnics took their place in mainstream American life. Italian Americans, for example, moved from the margins toward the center of national cultural and economic life. The Italian in "Italian American" became more a token of cultural heritage than a restricted economic niche. Given the enduring racial divide, the notion of a white identity became more apparent. As Italian Americans mainstreamed, white rather than Italian became a source of identity and political mobilization in many metropolitan areas.

The Immigration and Nationality Act of 1952 eliminated racial barriers to naturalization and immigration while also establishing a system of fixed quotas that favored northern and western Europeans. Amendments to this act in 1965 radically transformed immigration policy by abolishing national quotas and moving to a first-come, first-served system. Immigration policy was radically altered. The 1990 Immigration Act set a target of around 675,000 immigrants per year with preference for relatives of U.S. citizens as well as employment-based considerations that favor professional and skilled workers. The effect of the 1965 and 1990 legislation was to increase and broaden the migrant streams to the United States. In this second period, then, from the mid-1960s to the present day, immigration levels increased to more than 400,000 per year and surpassing a million per year in the early 1990s. In the first two decades of the 20th century the top five countries sending immigrants were, in order, Italy, Austria-Hungary, Russia, Canada, and the United Kingdom. In the last two decades the top five were Mexico, the Philippines, China and Taiwan, the Dominican Republic, and India.

The United States is an immigrant nation again. Between 1961 and 2000, more than 24 million immigrants were admitted to the United States. The percentage of foreign-born residents increased from 6.9 percent in 1950 to 11.1 percent in 2000. From 2000 to 2004 another 4.3 million immigrants arrived in the United States. Estimates now place the total number of immigrants at 34.2 million, or almost 12 percent of the total population. Table 5-1 highlights the main metropolitan destination points for foreign

Table 5-1.   Immigration and Metropolitan Areas, 2004

Metro area	Immigrants (thousands)	Percentage of total population
Los Angeles	5,507	31.9
New York	5,217	24.3
San Francisco	1,970	28.5
Miami-Dade	1,611	38.8
Chicago	1,370	15.4
Washington-Baltimore	1,281	15.4
Dallas	1,140	17.7
Houston	947	19.3
Boston	827	13.8
Seattle	524	14.2

migrants. The Los Angeles and New York metro areas have very large absolute amounts, followed by San Francisco, Miami-Dade, Chicago, and Baltimore-Washington. Three cities in Megalopolis feature in this top 10.

The large-scale immigration of the past 30 years converted a significant number of cities into multiethnic sites. New York City, for example, is the destination for almost 15 percent of all the new immigrants since 1965, and the city changed as the percentage of foreign-born residents exceeded 35 percent by 2000, a figure not achieved since 1910. The city is once again an immigrant city. The most recent wave of mass immigration transformed the look, feel, language, sounds, and smells of the largest cities. However, unlike the previous waves' concentration, there are wider spreads of immigrants throughout the metropolitan areas. Some settle in the central cities, but many of the more recent immigrants are widely scattered throughout the suburban areas of major metropolitan regions. Thus, whereas the Chinatowns of the 19th century were highly visible and dense, today's "little Koreas" are likely to be in suburban settings with people more widely dispersed, coming together for events such as weddings, dining, and shopping, rather than living together in tightly demarcated ethnic neighborhoods. If the early-20th-century immigration into the United States concentrated in the central areas, the early-21st-century immigration displays a distinctly more suburban metropolitan flavor.

In a recent study we were able to identify suburban places of significant immigration in 2000, designated as sites where more than 25 percent of the population was born overseas (Hanlon et al. 2006). Some of the suburban places had substantial foreign-born populations in 2000, such as Langley Park close to Washington, with 64.5 percent of its population born overseas.

IMMIGRATION IN MEGALOPOLIS

In 1960 the number of foreign-born people living in Megalopolis was around 4 million, constituting 10 percent of the region's total population. In 2000 the absolute and relative proportions had increased dramatically, such that by the century's end more than 10 million people in Megalopolis had been born overseas, and they constituted around 20 percent of the region's population, almost double the national average. Megalopolis attracted a considerable amount, in both absolute and relative terms, of the foreign immigration into the country. Almost one in two of all foreign-born people admitted to the United States since 1960 came to Megalopolis.

How are the immigrants distributed in Megalopolis? When we look at the distribution across the urban system, we can see the growing importance of the foreign-born people to central city populations (Table 5-2). By 2000 almost one in four of every central city resident had been born overseas, but even in the suburban areas of metropolitan regions there was a significant increase. In 1960 only two counties had a foreign-born population greater than 20 percent, Bronx (21.5 percent) and New York (22.1 percent). By 2000 16 counties had reached this figure; they included the traditional urban magnets of the Bronx and New York as well as more suburban counties, such as Fairfax County, Virginia, with 25.4 percent foreign born.

Table 5-3 shows the 10 counties with the highest percentages of immigrants in both 1960 and 2000 (Figures 5-1, 5-2, and 5-3). Three trends stand out. First, the traditional gateways for immigration in 1960 continued to attract immigrants in 2000. New York counties such as Bronx, Kings, Queens, and New York continue to act as magnets for the foreign-born. Second, new areas emerged in 2000, such as Montgomery County in Maryland and Alexandria City in Virginia, reflecting both the growth of the southern region of Megalopolis and the more suburban spread of the foreign born. Third, the number of immigrants increased both relatively and absolutely. Whereas the total number in the top 10 counties in 1960 was just over 2 million, by 2000 it had increased to 3.6 million.

The large, economically resilient urban regions, such as New York and Boston, have acted as powerful magnets for the foreign born, while more

Table 5-2.   Percentage Distribution of Foreign-born Residents in Megalopolis

	Percentage foreign born		
	1960	1980	2000
Central cities	14.1	14.2	24.8
Suburban counties	7.5	7.3	11.8

Table 5-3.   Top 10 Places for Foreign-born Residents in Megalopolis, 1960 and 2000

1960			2000		
County	Percentage	#	County	Percentage	#
New York, NY	22.1	375,320	Queens, NY	46.1	1,028,339
Bronx, NY	21.5	306,335	Hudson, NJ	38.5	234.597
Kings, NY	19.6	514,955	Kings, NY	37.8	931,769
Queens, NY	18.5	334,772	New York, NY	29.4	452,440
Suffolk, MA	15.5	122,656	Bronx, NY	29.0	385,827
Hudson, NJ	14.9	90,999	Arlington, VA	27.8	52,693
Passaic, NJ	14.9	60,586	Montgomery, MD	26.7	232,996
Westchester, NY	12.9	104,347	Passaic, NJ	26.1	130,291
Bristol, MA	12.4	49,413	Suffolk, MA	25.5	176,031
Hartford, CT	12.2	84,126	Alexandria, VA	25.4	32,600

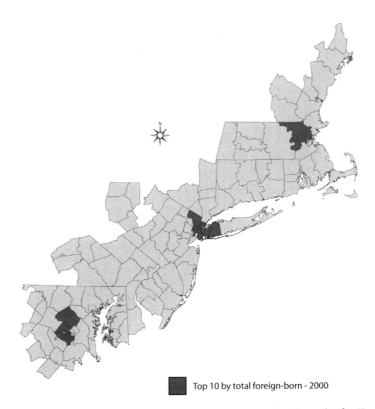

Top 10 by total foreign-born - 2000

Figure 5-1.   Distribution of the Foreign-born, 2000: Top Ten Counties by Number

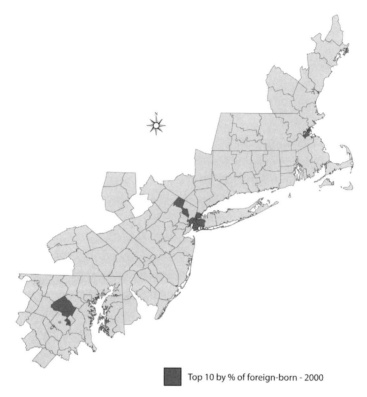

Top 10 by % of foreign-born - 2000

Figure 5-2.   Distribution of the Foreign-born, 2000: Top Ten Counties by Percent

economically challenged cities, such as Scranton, Pennsylvania, have been bypassed. Scranton had only 3.1 percent foreign born in 2000, which was less than half the 1960 figure of 6.5 percent. Baltimore City had 4.2 percent foreign born in 1960 and 4.6 percent in 2000; the numbers represent an absolute fall from 39,439 to 29,638. The presence of the foreign born is a good barometer of economic growth and decline.

The three primary areas for the foreign-born population in Megalopolis are the New York metro area, the Washington metro area, and Boston. Five New York counties—Bronx, Kings, Nassau, New York, and Westchester—account for 18.2 percent of the total population of Megalopolis, yet they house 38.6 percent of the total foreign-born people in Megalopolis. In Queens, New York, almost 1 of every 2 people is foreign born. Compare that statistic with Kentucky, where only 1 of every 50 was born overseas. Other New York counties, such as New York and Kings, have rates of 29.4 percent and 37.8 percent, respectively. The suburban counties surrounding the nation's capital are also major sites of immigration from overseas.

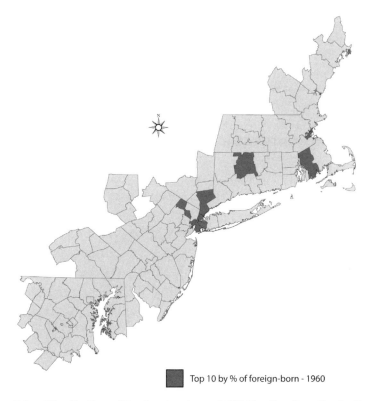

Top 10 by % of foreign-born - 1960

Figure 5-3.   Distribution of the Foreign-born, 1960: Top Ten Counties by Percent

Montgomery County, Maryland, has 26.7 percent foreign-born; Fairfax, Virginia, has 24.5 percent.

Within the region there is tremendous variation, from Queens, New York, with almost one in every two people, to Perry, Pennsylvania, with just less than one in a hundred. The more rural, less economically dynamic counties have low levels, such as Franklin, Massachusetts, with only 3.6 percent, and York, Maine, with 2.8 percent. Also, somewhat surprisingly, the growth counties in northern Virginia, such as Stafford and St. George, have only 4 percent and 1.3 percent, respectively. The in-migration of the native born rather than the foreign born fuels the growth of the suburbs of northern Virginia.

The proportion of the foreign born is a good indicator of economic growth because this group is more sensitive to variations in economic opportunities. They are attracted to places where jobs and economic opportunities are more readily available. Once established, the immigrant groups attract other immigrant groups. Their clustering in the three metro areas is a function of both better economic opportunities and the power of expatriate communities to attract subsequent immigrant flows. Immigrant enclaves, once established, become gateways for subsequent migrants and platforms for acculturation.

TWO MIGRANT STREAMS

The two largest racial and ethnic categories are Asian and Hispanic. There has been an Asian presence in selected cities of the United States for more than a hundred years. The oldest Asian enclaves are the traditional China-towns of New York and Philadelphia. From the 1960s, immigration from Asian countries expanded the Asian presence beyond the traditional centers of concentration. Asian immigration comprises a broad range of countries of origin, including Lebanon and Turkey as well as Laos and Thailand. The largest streams are from China, India, Korea, and the Philippines. Together, these four countries contribute more than 50 percent of Asian immigrants. New York has the largest absolute concentration of Asian population, 787,047 in 2000; the next largest city is Los Angeles, with 369,254. As with most migrant streams, Asians move toward the places where there are the most employment opportunities.

People who classified themselves as Asian in the census tend to come from a variety of educational backgrounds, but one important element is the preponderance of entrepreneurial and skilled workers among them. Al-though only 3.3 percent of Hispanics have advanced educational degrees, the comparable figure for Asians is 15.3 percent, and although 22.1 per-cent of African Americans live below the poverty line, only 10.8 percent of Asians do. Compared with the rest of the population, Asian migrants in general are better educated and more likely to own a business.

In Megalopolis two distinct clusters of Asians can be identified. First, the New York metro area stands out: Queens County, for example, has 391,500 Asian residents, or 17 percent, making it a significant Asian community. Large proportions of Asians reside in New York's suburban areas, such as Middlesex, New Jersey, with 104,212, or 13 percent. Asians are spread throughout the suburbs as well as the central city areas of selected metro-politan areas. A second concentration occurs around Washington. Fairfax, Virginia, for example, has 126,038, or 12 percent. Washington hosts a rela-tively small percentage; it is the city's expanding suburban areas that attract proportionately more Asians. A third, smaller concentration can be found in the Boston metro area. The Asian population is highly concentrated in these three metro areas, and away from them the population is small: Putnam, New York, for example, has about 1,000 Asians, or only 1.2 percent.

The number of Hispanics has been recorded only since the 1970 census, when a question on Spanish or Hispanic origin first appeared on the long form distributed to a sample of the population. In 1980 the Hispanic origin question was on the short form distributed to the entire population. The name itself is problematic: in recent years some complain of its European bias, preferring Latin or Latino/Latina to indicate a more New World emphasis. The term Latino/Hispanic is also a hybrid racial category because it includes both blacks and whites. In this chapter I use the term Hispanic while acknowledging its difficulties.

Since the 1980 census, the numbers of Hispanics rose in both relative and absolute amounts. This increase is in part a function of the census, which allows the designation of a Hispanic identity, as well as a function of increasing immigration from Central and South America. By 2000 almost 37 million people in the United States were designated Hispanic, constituting 13 percent of the national population. The largest national category of foreign born was Mexican, with 9.1 million, easily dwarfing the next four largest sources, Philippines (1.4 million), India (1 million), China (989,000), and Vietnam (988,000). The largest concentrations of Hispanics are found in the nation's three largest metro areas—New York, Los Angeles, and Chicago—with a significant representation in large cities in the West and Southwest of the country.

Just over 12 percent of the U.S. population is Hispanic. Megalopolis as a region has slightly less than the national average. Within Megalopolis the Hispanic population is concentrated in three metro areas. A small grouping is found around Boston, in Suffolk County (15.5 percent). In the Washington metro area there is a significant Hispanic population in northern Virginia: Arlington County (18.6 percent), Alexandria (14.7 percent), Fairfax County (13.6 percent), Manassas (15.1 percent), and Manassas Park (15 percent). The largest absolute and relative concentration is in the New York metro area. The largest single population concentration is in the Bronx with, according to the 2000 census, 644,705 people classified as Hispanics—almost one of every two people—and substantial populations are also found in Passaic, New Jersey (30 percent), Hudson, New Jersey (39.8 percent), Union, New Jersey (19.7 percent), New York (27.2 percent), and Kings (19.6 percent).

Throughout much of the rest of suburban and rural Megalopolis, the Hispanic population is small, apart from Cumberland, New Jersey (19 percent), and Hampden, Massachusetts (15.2 percent), whose high percentages are a function of past and present employment opportunities in agriculture and industry. The Hispanic presence pervades Megalopolis even in more rural areas, such as Washington, Maryland, where there are only 1,570 Hispanics in a total population of 131,923.

THE EFFECTS OF IMMIGRATION

Large-scale immigration into selected parts of Megalopolis has had profound effects (see Foner 2005, 2001; Waldinger 2001). Four are of particular importance. First, some areas of particularly high immigration have seen the creation of ethnic neighborhoods. In New York there are now three Chinatowns, a little Odessa, a Caribbean Brooklyn, and a Dominican Washington Heights. Whole areas have been transformed. Crown Heights in New York City has a definite Caribbean flavor. There are also extended immigrant communities that do not live together in the same neighborhood but meet for festivals and events. In suburban Washington, the Central and South American communities come together in Sunday soccer leagues. Different streams of immigrants have created more polyethnic neighborhoods, such as Queens in New York, which is one of the most diverse counties in the whole country, housing people from at least 50 different countries. Throughout Megalopolis, immigrants have changed the makeup of almost all counties, adding diversity and difference. Immigrants have played a role in revitalizing inner-city neighborhoods such as East Boston. In many cities the upturn in population since 1990 is due to foreign immigration. Soviet Jews, for example, brought vitality back to Brighton Beach in Brooklyn.

Second, racial and ethnic categories have been modified. The traditional division of black and white is replaced by a more fourfold structure of white, black, Asian, and Hispanic, and even the seemingly solid notions of black and white have been "tweaked," to use Vickerman's (2001) term, since "Hispanic" encompasses both black and white while Caribbean and African immigrants add a new twist to the idea of a singular black identity.

Third, immigrants have had a major impact on formal institutions, such as schools and churches. Public school enrollments in many cities have increased because of immigration, forcing issues of language proficiency to surface. In religion, the large Hispanic presence has given some inner-city Roman Catholic parishes a decidedly new flavor, and Korean churches dot the suburban landscape of selected counties, and mosques are beginning to appear.

Finally, not only have immigrants reshaped the job market, but also there are now identifiable ethnic employment niches in such areas as construction, health care, and higher education. The immigrant waves include the skilled and educated as well as the unskilled and ill-educated. At the low-wage end, the mass of immigrants has increased the supply of labor, making it more difficult for those at the bottom of the socioeconomic hierarchy, who lack skills to get employment. And as immigration continues, new ethnic entrepreneurs cater to the new communities, create links between entrepreneurs of similar ethnicity, and often connect the various homelands and diasporas through various economic transactions. We tend to think of economic globalization as something conducted mainly between huge transnational corporations, but it is also embodied in the flow of remittances from Megalopolis to Central American villages and in the trading links within family firms that connect China with Queens.

SUMMARY

The central region of the New York metro area, including the counties of Queens, Hudson, Kings, New York, and the Bronx, is the principal immigrant gateway in the region. In all five counties the foreign born constitute more than one in four of the population. Secondary gateways may be identified in the Boston area as well as the counties on the northern and western sides of the Washington metro area, including Montgomery, Maryland, and Arlington and Fairfax, Virginia. The more rural peripheral counties in the region—including Cumberland, Pennsylvania; Merrimack, New Hampshire; and Androscoggin, Maine—have very low levels of foreign-born residents.

The truly remarkable feature of this ethnic transformation is the extent to which the debate about changing national identity is, with a few notable exceptions, handled with extreme care in the public arena. The benefits of multiculturalism are widely proclaimed, and the trumpeting of the positive influences of a varied ethnic mix is now an integral part of mainstream, established political discourses. Nativist sentiments have gone underground to the realm of anecdotal gossip, sullen resentment, and a generally unarticulated sense that the country is "changing for the worse." Relatively few ethnic backlashes occur. The issue of illegal immigration is an organizing discourse for some anti-immigrant sentiment, but compared with much of the rest of the world, the United States in general and Megalopolis in particular have accommodated a profound change in the ethnic makeup of the country with remarkably few social tensions. In the United States the formal separation of church and state allows a rich religious diversity to blossom. The constitutional emphasis on individual rights rather than the elaboration of a singular ethnic identity is a fertile ground for the flourishing of a multiethnic society. The multinational population mix of Megalopolis has played a significant role in redefining the new demographic character of the United States. Metropolitan fluidity is also the less fixed and more elastic definition of what it means to be an American and a resident of Megalopolis.

CHAPTER SIX

PATTERNS OF SEGREGATION

Race and ethnicity are enduring features of social life in the United States. The basic question to be asked in this chapter is how the major racial and ethnic groups distribute themselves in Megalopolis. There are three problems in answering this question. The first involves the issue of data. Although the basic categorization of black and white has remained constant in the census since 1950 (and well before), questions about national identity have been asked only since 1970, and the identification of all people of Hispanic origin began only with the 1980 census. Race and ethnicity are as much social constructions as biological facts, and census categories often cloud an already complex issue. For example, categories in the 1950 census were White, Negro, American Indian, Japanese, Chinese, and Filipino—an awkward combination of racial types, ethnicities, and nationalities. Hispanics can still be counted as either black or white. Racial categories are more a product of changing census definitions than constant physical facts: they are complex amalgams rather than simple categories. The groupings I use, based on census classifications, are designed to give us commonly accepted categories. I will look at four main racial and ethnic groupings: blacks, whites, Asians, and Hispanics. The groups are not homogeneous. Neither are they all-encompassing. The number of Native Americans, for example, is so small as to make analysis difficult. Nor are these categories "scientific" or "natural" divisions. They are social constructions, but important social constructions nonetheless.

Since in 1950 the Census Bureau used enumerators' choices for racial categorization, the data are not comparable with those from later censuses. I will therefore take the 1960 census as the base point for analysis. Data on blacks and whites will be used for 1960, 1980, and 2000 and estimated for Asians. For the 1960 data the estimated Asian population consists of Japanese, Chinese, and Filipino, and for 1980, Japanese, Chinese, Filipino, Korean, and Vietnamese. For 2000 the Census Bureau has a specific Asian category that is based on the self-identification of people of "Asian descent." Data on Hispanics will be used from 1980 through 2000.

For each of the four groups—blacks, whites, Asians, and Hispanics— similar techniques will be used. Indices of segregation and dissimilarity will be calculated to obtain measures of segregation over time, and location quotients will also be calculated and then mapped to show areas of minority concentration. This empirical analysis allows the identification of changing patterns of segregation as well as the evolution of residential concentrations of minorities.

The second problem in answering the basic question is the issue of scale. Indices of segregation are acutely sensitive to scale (Wong 2003). We can demonstrate this with reference to 2000 racial data for Washington, D.C. For the entire Washington area the percentage of nonwhites is 69.2 percent. At the zip code level the average figure drops to 56.1 percent, but at the level of census tract it increases to 72.4 percent (Wong 2004). In an ideal world of unlimited resources the indices would be calculated for the different scales of counties, census places, and census tracts. Given real-world constraints, however, the analysis will be restricted to the coarse-grained county level. Previous research indicates that the finer the scale, the greater the degree of segregation. Segregation is most marked at the more local neighborhood level. Analysis at the county level tends to underestimate the degree of segregation.

The third problem is that the census categories refer only to residence. The census figures are like population counts in the middle of the night when everyone is, or at least should be, at home. During the day, however, we travel to work, journey to school, and weave complex space-time paths across the urban landscape. Segregation indices refer to residences and not to the more complex patterns of interaction that we negotiate during the day. Although we may not live beside people of a different race or ethnic-

Table 6-1. Percentage Distribution of Racial and Ethnic Groups in United States and Megalopolis

	White	Black	Asian	Hispanic
1960	88.5 (89.9)	10.5 (9.8)	0.5 (0.2)	–
1980	85.9 (82.9)	11.9 (14.1)	1.6 (1.1)	6.4 (6.2)
2000	80.8 (77.8)	12.7 (16.8)	3.8 (5.3)	12.9 (12.0)

Note: Figures for Megalopolis are in parentheses. Rows do not add up to 100 in 1960 because of other categories and double-counting of Hispanics in the categories of black and white in 1980 and 2000.

ity, we may interact with them during the normal course of a working day. Residence-based population data are partial but still important.

Table 6-1 summarizes the relevant aggregate information. In 1960 both the nation and Megalopolis were overwhelmingly white: 9 of every 10 persons were classified as white. By 2000, 8 of every 10 people in the country were considered white. The difference was a growth in the proportion of blacks, Asians, and Hispanics. Megalopolis is slightly more racially and ethnically diverse than the rest of the country. The black and Asian populations have increased in Megalopolis more than in the rest of the nation while the Hispanic population reflects the national average. From 1960 to 2000 Megalopolis diversified with more blacks, Asians, and Hispanics. Table 6-2 shows the changes in absolute numbers from 1960 to 2000. While the white population remained approximately constant, at around 34 million, the black population doubled to just over 7.5 million, and the Asian population had the greatest increase, from a tiny 87,000 to a substantial 2.3 million. There were almost 6 million Hispanics in Megalopolis in 2000. The increase in the population of Megalopolis from 1960 to 2000 was in part due to the increase in the number of nonwhites.

Higher levels of immigration increased the proportion of Asians and Hispanics. From 1950 to the mid-1960s, immigration was limited. Immigration policy was transformed by 1965 amendments to the Immigration and Nationality Act of 1952, which abolished national quotas and moved to a first-come, first-served system and inaugurated a period of increased immigration. Emphasis was placed on family reunification, and this meant that citizens with families overseas had preference, with no restriction placed on the numbers coming from any one country. Large families, especially marked in Asian and Hispanic households, were thus guaranteed increased

Table 6-2. Racial and Ethnic Populations (thousands) in Megalopolis

	White	Black	Asian	Hispanic
1960	33,383	3,654	869	na
2000	34,805	7,528	2,381	5,846

access. Between 1971 and 1980, 4.5 million immigrants came to the United States, with increasing numbers coming from Asia and Latin America. From the mid-1960s, immigrants exceeded 400,000 per year, surpassing 1 million per year in the early 1990s. In the period from 1971 to 1995, 17.1 million immigrants came to the United States. The most common countries of origin were Mexico, the Philippines, China and Taiwan, the Dominican Republic, and India. The migrant stream now included more Asians and Hispanics.

Although some of the increase in the black population is due to immigration, as migrants move from Africa and the Caribbean, it is also due to internal migration, as blacks moved from the rural South to the urban Northeast. From the late 1940s to the mid-1970s, there was substantial migration of blacks from rural to urban and from South to North. From the mid-1960s, there was massive population redistribution as almost 5 million blacks from the southern states made their way to the cities in the North, driven by a search for social freedom and better economic opportunities. People left the cotton fields for the inner-city neighborhoods, and a predominantly rural population became more urban. As blacks moved into some urban neighborhoods, whites moved out, and as more whites moved out, more blacks moved in. Racial prejudices and outright discrimination herded the incoming black population into the poorest neighborhoods, where houses were subdivided and further subdivided to meet the increased demand. Complex patterns of housing discrimination, involving steering by real estate agents and lending by banks, restricted African American households to "black" areas of the city.

MEASURING SEGREGATION

Although the aggregate numbers of racial and ethnic groups are important, it is necessary to examine their internal distribution. In 1960, both the central cities and suburban districts were overwhelmingly white. Since then, the central cities have become more multiracial. More than 83 percent of the central city population was white in 1960, but the figure was only 42 percent by 2000. Suburbs also have become more multiracial. In 1960, 96 percent of the suburban population was white, but by 2000 this figure had fallen to 78 percent. In 1960, the white population was almost evenly split between metro core and suburbs—1 of every 2 white people lived in a central city—but by 2000, this figure had fallen to 2 in 10 (Table 6-3).

Table 6-3.   Racial and Ethnic Percentage Distribution by Central City and Suburbs

	White	Black	Asian	Hispanic
1960				
Central city	83.8	15.7	0.3	–
Suburbs	96.2	3.7	0.1	–
1980				
Central city	69.8	22.5	1.4	10.6
Suburbs	90.7	6.8	0.7	2.5
2000				
Central city	42.6	27.4	7.4	20.3
Suburbs	78.7	9.5	4.4	6.8

Note: Rows do not add up to 100 percent in 1980 and 2000 because of other categories and double-counting of Hispanics in the categories of black and white in 1980 and 2000.

We can consider the patterns of segregation more specifically by using the index of segregation (IS). The IS is a widely used measure that compares the distribution of a subgroup to the total population, expressed as a value from 1 to 100. IS values closer to 100 indicate a greater degree of residential segregation.

Table 6-4 lists the segregation index for the four main groups. We can interpret them using the index example of 43.3 percent for whites in 1960. The figure means that 43.3 percent of whites would have to move to another area to achieve the same distribution as the total population. This is a high value, indicating marked segregation.

The high values shown in Table 6-4 indicate consistently pronounced levels of segregation for all the groups. Whites and blacks were more segregated in 1980 than in 1960, then returned to their 1960 pattern in 2000. These data can be interpreted as reflecting the differential nature of suburbanization until 1980: as blacks were moving into the central cities, whites were moving out to the suburbs. The 1980 values indicate the high-water mark of this trend. The 2000 values reflect the greater suburbanization of blacks and consequently slightly less segregation. Segregation of Asians remained approximately the same, while Hispanics became slightly less segregated in 2000 compared with 1980, in part because of the wider suburban spread of Hispanics through Megalopolis. In conclusion, all the groups exhibit high degrees of segregation at the county level, with the most marked and in-

Table 6-4.   Index of Segregation in Megalopolis

	White	Black	Asian	Hispanic
1960	43.3	43.8	37.8	na
1980	51.2	48.4	35.1	48.4
2000	40.8	42.6	34.2	38.0

Table 6-5.   Index of Segregation for Census Tracts in Selected Counties, 2000

County	IS value for whites
Baltimore County, MD	49.3
Bergen, NJ	38.5
Burlington, NJ	44.8
Dauphin, PA	37.8
Middlesex, CT	31.7
Montgomery, MD	23.2
Prince George's, MD	57.2
Megalopolis	40.8

creasing patterns of segregation for the white and black populations. Remember that we are using county data, so segregation is even more marked at the finer-grained level of neighborhoods and census tracts. But even at this coarse-grained county level, the high degree of segregation is striking. We have talked about the liquid metropolis, but in terms of race and ethnicity, continuing segregation is a stubbornly solid fact of metropolitan stability.

To check the effects of scale, IS values are also calculated for whites in 2000 in 10 census tracts chosen randomly from 7 counties, also randomly chosen. The data shown in Table 6-5 reveal a scatter around the regional value of 40.8 and reinforce the point that the regional value is an average that covers a wide fluctuation of values, indicating both more pronounced and less marked segregation.

We can also compare the segregation between pairs of racial and ethic groups through the index of dissimilarity (ID), which is similar to the index of segregation in that it uses the percentage of each of two groups in different areas to calculate a value from 1 to 100. This value is the percentage of the population that would have to move to have a spatial spread similar to the other group. Table 6-6 shows the index for all pairs of groups from 1960 to 2000. The dissimilarity in the spatial spread of blacks and whites remains consistently high. In fact, the index for 2000 is higher than it was in 1960, which is a staggering finding given the decline of many of the formal and

Table 6-6.   Index of Dissimilarity in Megalopolis

	Index of dissimilarity		
	1960	1980	2000
Whites/Blacks	43.9	49.9	47.1
Whites/Asians	39.5	38.2	39.2
Whites/Hispanics	na	49.3	42.3
Blacks/Asians	40.2	42.2	41.2
Blacks/Hispanics	na	37.5	36.2
Asians/Hispanics	na	32.9	29.6

Table 6-7.   Index of Dissimilarity for Census Tracts in Selected Counties, 2000

County	ID value for whites and blacks
Baltimore County, MD	54.1
Bergen, NJ	57.9
Burlington, NJ	51.4
Dauphin, PA	49.5
Middlesex, CT	39.4
Montgomery, MD	26.8
Prince George's, MD	62.1
Megalopolis	47.1

explicit practices of racial discrimination. A striking feature is the persistently high indices for all the groups. For only one pair, Asians and Hispanics, did the index fall below 30, perhaps because more recent immigrants live in the same neighborhoods. The data reveal persistent segregation between all the groups; increased segregation between blacks and whites from 1960 to 2000; stable and high levels for whites and Asians, blacks and Asians, as well as blacks and Hispanics; and a slight decline in segregation levels between whites and Hispanics and between Asians and Hispanics.

Table 6-7 shows the ID values for whites and blacks for the same 7 randomly selected census tracts and counties as in Table 6-5. And again, a wide scatter of values is apparent, with some very marked patterns of segregation.

Although the indices of segregation and dissimilarity measure aggregate patterns of spatial distribution, they do not identify areas of concentration. This can be examined in two ways. First, concentration can be measured by the location quotient (LQ), which is calculated by dividing the percentage of the subgroup in an area by the percentage of the total population in the same area. LQ values of less than 1 indicate areas of underrepresentation, and values greater than 1 indicate overrepresentation; the larger the LQ, the greater the concentration of the subgroup. Second, we can identify areas of greatest absolute concentration. We will weigh both of these approaches by considering each of the racial and ethnic groups.

WHITES

In 1960 whites were spread evenly throughout Megalopolis, and LQ values clustered around 1, with a minimum value of 0.66 in Calvert County, Maryland, and a maximum of 1.11 in Merrimack, New Hampshire. By 2000, the values had widened, with a minimum value of 1.35 in Carbon County,

Pennsylvania, and a maximum of 0.37 in Prince George's County, Mary-land. The spatial pattern of LQ values shows a relative decline in the white population in the large urban centers and a relative increase in the outer suburbs of the region. These patterns are summarized in Figure 6-1, which shows the LQ values in terms of degrees of standard deviation from the mean. This statistic allows us to compare values more easily. The pattern revealed in Figure 6.1 is indicative of white flight from the central cities.

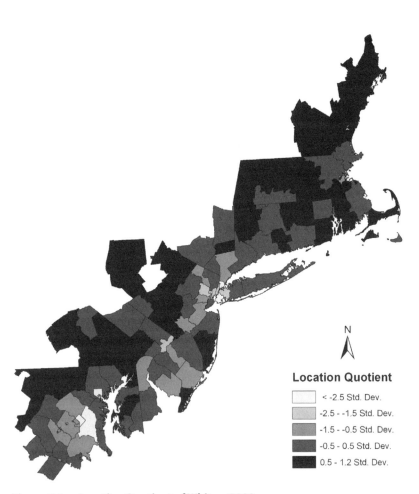

Figure 6-1.   Location Quotient of Whites, 2000

BLACKS

The reverse pattern is shown for the black population. LQ values in 1960 were wide, from 0.002 in Perry County, Pennsylvania, to 5.48 in the District of Columbia. By 2000 the range of values had shrunk somewhat, from 0.028 in Perry County to 4.16 in Baltimore City. There was an increased but thin spread of blacks throughout the region and increased concentration in selected cities and suburbs. Figure 6-2 shows the LQ values in 2000, by standard deviation, and reveals increased concentration in the urban centers and the inner suburban areas around the largest cities. Table 6-8 lists the counties with the largest concentrations. The large urban centers dominate this picture.

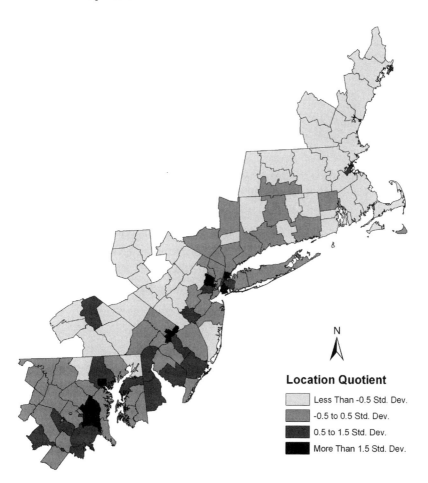

Location Quotient

	Less Than -0.5 Std. Dev.
	-0.5 to 0.5 Std. Dev.
	0.5 to 1.5 Std. Dev.
	More Than 1.5 Std. Dev.

Figure 6-2.   Location Quotient of Blacks, 2000

Table 6-8. Top 20 Counties with Highest Percentage of Black Population

	1960			2000	
	Counties	%		Counties	%
DC	Washington	53.90	MD	Baltimore City	64.34
MD	Calvert	42.13	MD	Prince George's	62.70
MD	Baltimore City	34.67	DC	Washington	60.01
MD	Charles	33.26	PA	Philadelphia	43.22
VA	Culpepper	27.43	NJ	Essex	41.24
MD	Talbot	27.12	NY	Kings	36.44
VA	King George	26.92	NY	Bronx	35.64
MD	Queen Anne's	26.91	MD	Charles	26.06
PA	Philadelphia	26.43	VA	Alexandria City	22.54
MD	Kent	26.15	MA	Suffolk	22.24
VA	Fauquier	25.92	NJ	Union	20.78
NY	New York	23.38	DE	Kent	20.66
VA	Spotsylvania	22.81	VA	Fredericksburg	20.41
MD	Caroline	20.18	DE	New Castle	20.22
NJ	Essex	19.57	NJ	Cumberland	20.20
VA	Fredericksburg	19.01	MD	Baltimore	20.10
VA	Loudoun	17.66	NY	Queens	20.01
NJ	Atlantic	17.54	NJ	Mercer	19.81
VA	Clarke	17.20	VA	Prince William	18.76
WV	Jefferson	15.44	VA	King George	18.73

Table 6-9 shows an increasing concentration of blacks in selected large cities over the period 1950 to 2000. This process occurred in traditionally black cities, such as Baltimore, as well as cities with relatively small black populations in 1950, such as Boston. In effect, the central cities became increasingly black both in absolute and in relative terms. The one exception was Washington, which was a majority black city by 1970 after the precipitous white flight of the 1950s and 1960s: by 2000 Washington had experienced a relative decline in the black population.

The black migration to the cities of Megalopolis was part of a long tradition of minority groups moving to the central city. Other groups also had a hard time in a white Protestant country: the Irish, Italians, and Jews originally all faced hostility and discrimination. But while the other groups left the city for the suburbs, the blacks tended to remain. Institutionalized racism was different from ethnic hostility. Blacks were formally discriminated against in a housing market that restricted their housing choices.

At the midpoint of the 20th century, the rural landscape was the dominant backdrop for representation of black identity in the United States. At the beginning of the 21st century, blacks had become urbanized and cities became racially diverse. As blacks moved into the central cities, the

Table 6-9.   Black Populations in Central Cities

City	Percentage		
	1950	1970	2000
Baltimore	23.8	46.4	64.3
Boston	5.3	16.3	25.3
New York City	9.8	21.1	26.6
Philadelphia	18.1	33.6	43.2
Washington	35.0	71.1	60.9

good blue-collar jobs started to suburbanize. The long deindustrialization of central city America began just after the blacks moved there. The declining fiscal health of the cities, in part a function of the job loss, also made it difficult to provide the range of services, especially education, that enabled the next generation to move up and out. Funnels of failures were created in central city America.

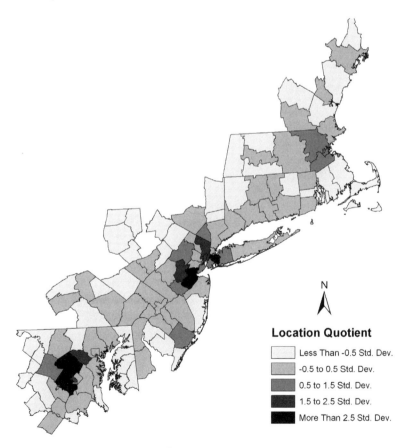

Figure 6-3.   Location Quotient of Asians, 2000

ASIANS

The category used here is a Census classification that includes recent immi grants from Asia as well as Asian Americans who have lived in this country for generations. In 1960 there were relatively few Asians in Megalopolis, and most of them were highly concentrated. LQ values ranged from 0 in Jefferson, West Virginia, to 6.4 in New York County. There was a distinct clustering in the three largest metro areas, Boston and particularly New York and Washington. From 1960 to 2000, the numbers increased, and there was a wider spread throughout the region; by 2000, the LQ values ranged from 0.03 in Litchfield, Vermont, to 3.5 in Queens, New York. The 1960 values represent a small Asian population concentrated in traditional Chinatowns, whereas the 2000 values reflect a more widespread Asian pres ence (Figure 6-3). Table 6-10 also reveals the changing pattern, listing the top 20 Asian places in 1960 and 2000. Notice how the absolute figures have increased dramatically. In 1960 the Asian presence was limited to Chi natown in New York City. By 2000, after almost four decades of sustained immigration from Asia, the absolute numbers had increased dramatically

Table 6-10.   Top 20 Counties with Highest Percentage of Asian Population

	1960			2000	
	Counties	*%*		*Counties*	*%*
NY	New York	1.50	NY	Queens	17.56
NJ	Cumberland	0.65	NJ	Middlesex	13.88
DC	Washington	0.61	VA	Fairfax	13.00
MA	Suffolk	0.54	VA	Fairfax City	12.17
NJ	Burlington	0.47	MD	Montgomery	11.30
RI	Newport	0.41	NJ	Bergen	10.67
MD	Montgomery	0.40	NY	New York	9.40
NY	Queens	0.39	NJ	Hudson	9.35
MD	Prince George's	0.37	VA	Arlington	8.62
MD	Anne Arundel	0.35	NJ	Somerset	8.38
CT	New London	0.30	MD	Howard	7.68
VA	Falls Church	0.29	NY	Kings	7.54
VA	Fairfax	0.29	MA	Suffolk	7.00
VA	Arlington	0.27	VA	Falls Church	6.50
NY	Kings	0.25	NJ	Morris	6.26
VA	Alexandria City	0.25	MA	Middlesex	6.26
RI	Washington	0.24	VA	Alexandria City	5.65
NJ	Monmouth	0.23	NY	Richmond	5.65
MD	Harford	0.22	NY	Rockland	5.52
NY	Westchester	0.20	MA	Norfolk	5.50

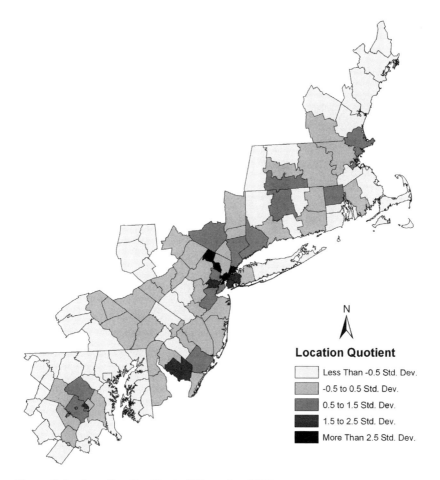

Figure 6-4.   Location Quotient of Hispanics, 2000

and Asian Americans have spread to selected suburban counties in the economic growth zones of Megalopolis.

HISPANICS

The Hispanic category is a category of origin rather than race, since it includes people who could classify themselves as either black or white. The
question about Hispanic origin was first asked of the whole U.S. population in 1980, when just over 6 percent of the total classified themselves
as Hispanic in both Megalopolis and the nation as a whole. By 2000, this

figure had doubled, with the national figure slightly larger than the figure for Megalopolis. In 1980, the LQ values ranged from 0.06 in Luzerne, Pennsylvania, to 4.21 in Hudson, New Jersey, indicating a heavy concentration in only a few areas. By 2000, the values ranged from a minimum of 0.0005 in Suffolk, New York, to a maximum of 3.61 in Hudson, New Jersey, with the distribution of values overall suggesting a continuing concentration in selected areas but a wider spread throughout the region. Figure 6-4 shows a marked concentration in the New York metro area and the inner-ring growth suburbs of Washington as well as Boston. In the rest of the region, there is a thin spread. The Hispanic population is concentrated in selected metro regions.

Table 6-11 lists the counties with highest percentage of Hispanics. While traditional areas of Hispanic immigration, such as the Bronx and Hudson, Passaic, and New York counties, have increased their relative and absolute numbers, there are now significant Hispanic populations in the suburban counties of Westchester, New York, and Manassas, Virginia.

Table 6-11.   Top 20 Counties with Highest Percentage of Hispanic Population

	1980			2000	
	Counties	%		Counties	%
NY	Bronx	33.91	NY	Bronx	48.38
NY	Hudson	26.06	NJ	Hudson	39.76
NY	New York	23.54	NJ	Passaic	29.95
NY	Kings	17.58	NY	New York	27.18
NJ	Passaic	13.88	NY	Queens	24.97
NY	Queens	13.88	NY	Kings	19.79
NJ	Cumberland	9.43	NJ	Union	19.71
NJ	Essex	8.99	NJ	Cumberland	19.00
NJ	Union	8.09	VA	Arlington	18.81
MA	Suffolk	6.16	NY	Westchester	15.61
VA	Arlington	5.81	MA	Suffolk	15.52
NJ	Middlesex	5.73	NJ	Essex	15.42
CT	Fairfield	5.59	MA	Hampden	15.17
NY	Richmond	5.36	VA	Manassas	15.13
NY	Westchester	5.26	VA	Manassas Park	15.00
MA	Hampden	5.13	VA	Alexandria City	14.72
CT	Hartford	5.13	VA	Fairfax City	13.64
NY	Suffolk	4.57	NJ	Middlesex	13.58
NY	Rockland	4.54	RI	Providence	13.39
NJ	Camden	4.37	NJ	Atlantic	12.17

METRO-LEVEL CHANGE

Our analysis is restricted to the county level. An analysis by Fasenfest et al. (2004) was undertaken at the finer-grained level of the census tract. They look at changing racial and ethnic composition from 1990 to 2000 and show that the number of predominantly white tracts, those with more than 80 percent whites, declined across metro areas, as did the number of predominantly black tracts, those with at least 50 percent blacks, while the number of mixed-race tracts increased. I have represented their data for the four metro areas in Megalopolis in Table 6-12. Boston and Philadelphia still have a majority of tracts that are predominantly white despite the increase in mixed-race tracts, and in New York and Washington, around two-thirds of all census tracts are classified as mixed race. Across the metro areas of Megalopolis, there has been a very marked increase in the number of mixed-race tracts.

SUMMARY

We can summarize the results in terms of racial and ethnic categories as well as in terms of places. The white population is still the dominant group in the region. The absolute numbers remained relatively static from 1960 to 2000. The population growth in Megalopolis has been fueled by nonwhites, with the result that the white population has declined in relative terms to less than 78 percent of the total, down from 88.5 percent in 1960. Whites have redistributed from the central cities to the suburbs. In 1960, 83.8 percent of the population of the central cities was white, but by 2000 this had declined to 42.4 percent. Whites became less urban and more suburban. In some of the more rural counties in the south of the region with a historical black presence, there was a relative and absolute increase in the white population. Calvert County, Maryland, for example, has a substantial black population, the descendants of freed slaves who had established tobacco farms as well as fished for oysters. In 1960, the black population of 6,667 accounted for 42.1 percent of the county's population. Calvert was a predominantly rural place in southern Maryland, far from the metropolitan scenes of Washington and Baltimore. Fast forward to 2000, and the black population of 9,773 was only 13.1 percent of the county population. As white suburbanites moved farther out on the tide of the liquid metropolis, the black population became a minority. House prices have increased, and

Table 6-12.   Census Tract Race Classification in Megalopolis, 2000

Metro area	Percentage of census tracts	
Boston	Predominantly white	55.7
	Predominantly black	0.6
	Mixed race	42.1
New York	Predominantly white	9.4
	Predominantly black	8.9
	Mixed race	69.0
Philadelphia	Predominantly white	55.0
	Predominantly black	12.7
	Mixed race	32.0
Washington	Predominantly white	16.1
	Predominantly black	18.7
	Mixed race	64.2

Source: Based on data in Fasenfest et al. (2004).

many locals have felt marginalized and ignored as the county becomes a typical white outer suburb. In 2005, of the five-member board of county commissioners, four were white, all born outside the county (Paley 2005).

Blacks have doubled in population from 1960 to 2000 and now constitute 16.8 percent of the region's population. In 1960, blacks constituted 15.7 percent of the central city population; by 2000, this figure had increased to 27.4 percent. They have become the majority population, especially in cities that have witnessed job and population loss. Take the case of Philadelphia, which had a population of just over 2 million in 1960, a quarter of them black. By 2000, the total population had declined to 1.5 million, 655,581 classified as black. The population loss was predominantly of white people, which meant an increasing proportion of blacks. A similar pattern emerges for smaller cities. New Haven, Connecticut, and Wilmington, Delaware, for example, both saw a steady decline in population and a rise in the black population to 37 percent and 56 percent, respectively, over the 40-year period. White flight has left proportionately more blacks in the central cities, especially the cities experiencing greatest economic difficulties.

There has also been black suburbanization. In 1960, there were 773,160 blacks in the suburbs of Megalopolis, but by 2000, this number had climbed to almost 3 million. Prince George's in Maryland, for example, a county that borders Washington's predominantly black Northeast and Southeast quadrants, has a majority black population. It is home to more than half a million blacks, who constitute two of every three people in the county.

The Asian population in Megalopolis has increased from a relatively insignificant 87,000 to more than 2.3 million. Asians are found in the central cities as well as the suburbs. Their numbers are significant at the very local level but have yet to reach a critical mass sufficient for a significant county power base.

There are now almost 6 million Hispanics in Megalopolis, constituting 12 percent of the total population. Three-fifths are in the central cities, the remainder in the suburbs. The growth is particularly marked in the major metro areas of New York, Washington, and Boston. In selected cities and counties, the Hispanic population has been the major driver of demographic growth.

Whites have become more suburbanized; blacks have also suburbanized, but a significant majority remains in the central city. Asians and Hispanics have become a more pervasive presence across the region, especially in the more economically buoyant cities and inner-ring suburbs. The more distant suburbs are white, the inner-ring suburbs are more polyethnic, and the central cities have become more nonwhite. Table 6-13 presents data that both summarizes and highlights the trends for three counties that cut a transect across the region from a largely black central city (Philadelphia) to a diversifying inner-ring suburb (Alexandria) to a more distant suburb that is becoming more white (Calvert).

Although change has been a significant feature of the racial and ethnic population redistribution, we should also note the remarkable stability of the indices, which indicates an underlying pattern of persistent segregation. And there has been stasis as well as change. Newport County, Rhode Island has also been added to the table. The county saw a population increase from 81,891 in 1960 to 87,194 in 2000. However, the white population shifted only slightly, from 95 percent to 91.5 percent. The increase in population was due not to more blacks, whose numbers declined from 3,593 to 3,184, but to more Asians and Hispanics. But the city remained overwhelmingly white. Change and stability, redistribution with persistent segregation: Megalopolis exhibits both the remarkable changes in the racial and ethnic distribution of population as well as the obdurate, granitelike stabilities.

Table 6-13.   White Population in Selected Counties

	Percentage	
	1960	*2000*
Philadelphia	73.2	45.0
Alexandria, VA	88.3	59.8
Calvert, MD	57.8	83.9
Newport, RI	95.0	91.5

CHAPTER SEVEN

COUNTY DIVERSITY

S
o far we have been looking at individual counties in relation to a range of characteristics. But it is also useful to identify differences between counties. In this chapter I want to identify broad categories of counties within Megalopolis. Counties are large, and the larger the number of observations in a unit, the greater the possible range. Take household median income. The median household income for Prince George's County, Maryland, in 1999 was $55,256. But this is an average across approximately 286,600 households, some of whom will have very much more and others very much less. We should always bear this range in mind when we use counties as single observations.

The aggregate nature of the county data precludes a very sophisticated analysis. This will be attempted in the next chapter when we use the finer-grained census place data. For the moment I will choose two variables that provide a simple matrix to classify the counties. An obvious first choice is income, since it is a primary source of economic power and social difference. In particular I will use median household income. Variations in household income embody and reflect the more basic differences between people and places in Megalopolis. Income is such a primary source of difference that most other variables correlate highly with it, making them redundant as other sources of analytical differentiation. One exception is the number of foreign-born residents, since relatively high percentages are found in both rich and poor areas. The two variables combined give us a measure of income and what I will call cosmopolitanism. The higher the median county income, the more affluent the county, and the more immigrants there are, the more cosmopolitan. The term cosmopolitan does not imply that all households in the county will have a "cosmopolitan" lifestyle or that they are necessarily affected by the foreign-born people in their midst. At the county scale this is making monumental assumptions because of the issue of the size of counties, already alluded to, as well as what is referred to as the "ecological fallacy," which states that we cannot draw conclusions about individuals from aggregate data. The term cosmopolitan, as used here, simply refers to the *presence* in the county of immigrants rather than the *consequences* of their presence.

INCOME AND IMMIGRANTS

The median household income in 1999 across the region was $51,897, making Megalopolis one of the more affluent parts of the United States. The national figure is $41,994. In reality, of course, there is substantial variation within the region. A belt of affluence stretches through the suburban counties from southern Virginia through Maryland and New Jersey up to New York and into New England. Counties within the central portion of this belt include Fairfax, Virginia ($81,050), Howard, Maryland ($74,167), Morris, New Jersey ($77,340), Rockland, New York ($67,971), Fairfield, Connecticut ($65,249), and Norfolk, Massachusetts ($63,432), which all have median household incomes well above the regional and national figures. Within this suburban band of affluence there are the pockets of relative poverty in central cities, such as Baltimore ($30,078), Philadelphia ($30,746), and the Bronx ($27,611). Lower median incomes are also found in the declining industrial regions of Pennsylvania and New England, where counties such as Lackawanna, Pennsylvania ($34,438), and Providence, Rhode Island ($36,950), have household income levels below the regional and national levels. Surrounding the belt of affluence are the more rural or older industrial, peripheral counties of the region, such as Caroline, Maryland ($38,832), and Perry, Pennsylvania ($41,409), which fall just below the national average. There is substantial variation in median income across

Megalopolis and a resulting world of difference between on the one hand suburban affluence and on the other urban poverty and industrial decline.

Since the 1970s there has been a revival of immigration to levels last seen in the early 1920s. In the past 30 years there has been an increase in the number of people born overseas but now living in the United States. Just over 1 of every 10 people in the United States was born in another country. Megalopolis is one of the major destination points for the foreign born. The three primary areas of foreign-born population are the New York metro area, the suburbs of Washington, and Boston (see Chapter 5).

A TYPOLOGY OF COUNTIES

We can combine the two variables in a simple matrix. Figure 7-1 displays the categorization using the quartile divisions of each variable. Plotting the distribution of each county along the two variables thus provides a

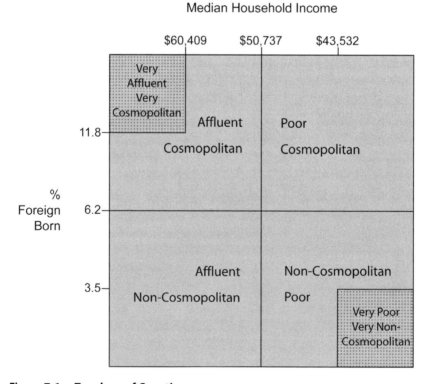

Figure 7-1. Typology of Counties

possible 16-cell classification. Combining similar cells provides a sixfold classification of counties based on their degree of affluence and percentage of foreign-born residents. The resulting classification in Table 7-1 lists the counties, median household income, and foreign-born percentage of each group. The categories are mapped in Figures 7-2a and b.

The *very affluent, very cosmopolitan* counties have a median household income of more than $60,409 and a foreign-born population greater than 11.8 percent. This favored category of counties is located in the suburban districts of the Washington, New York, and Boston metro areas. They house the more affluent households working in the dynamic growth sectors of producer services, including finance (especially in New York and Boston) and scientific and government-related research (especially around Washington and Boston). These are the white-collar brain industries that attract workers from around the world as well as provide them with enough disposable income to pay for ancillary service workers, such as nannies, also often from overseas. A typical county in this category is Montgomery County, Maryland, which has a median household income of $71,551 with 20.7 percent foreign born. Located in the Washington metro area, which has experienced major employment growth because of the federal government, Montgomery County is home to the National Institutes of Health and numerous other government research establishments that provide steady, well-paying jobs. There is an important biomedical research corridor alongside Interstate 270 from Bethesda to Rockville that recruits from a global labor pool.

The second category, the *affluent cosmopolitan* counties, includes very affluent counties such as Hunterdon, New Jersey, with a median income of $79,888 but only 6.3 percent foreign born, as well as very cosmopolitan counties such as New York, with 29.4 percent foreign born but a median income of only $57,030. This category includes both affluent suburban counties and cosmopolitan urban counties, some of which are very similar to the very affluent, very cosmopolitan. Loudoun County, Virginia, for example, has a median household income of $80,648 and 11.3 percent foreign born, and then the category drifts toward the less affluent, less cosmopolitan, such as Plymouth, Massachusetts with a median income of $55,615 and only 6.3 percent foreign born. This category of counties, like the first, is located around the central primary metro area corridor that runs from Washington through New York to Boston.

Although we often associate affluence with owner-occupied housing, there are at least three counties in the two affluent categories with relatively low levels of owner occupation. Arlington County and the city of

Table 7-1.   County Typology

	Household income	Percentage foreign born	State	County
Very affluent, very cosmopolitan	$67,146	14.8	CT	Fairfield
			MA	Middlesex, Norfolk
			MD	Montgomery
			NJ	Bergen, Middlesex, Monmouth, Morris, Somerset
			NY	Nassau, Rockland, Suffolk, Westchester
			VA	*Arlington*, Fairfax City, Fairfax, Falls Church, Manassas, Manassas Park, Prince William
Affluent cosmopolitan	$59,115	11.2	CT	Hartford
			DE	New Castle
			MA	Essex, Nantucket, Plymouth
			MD	Harford, Howard, Prince George's
			NH	Hillsborough
			NJ	Burlington, Camden, Hunterdon, Mercer, Union
			NY	Dutchess, *New York*, Orange, Putnam, Richmond
			PA	Montgomery
			RI	Bristol
			VA	*Alexandria*, Loudoun, Stafford
Poor cosmopolitan	$42,298	17.0	CT	New Haven
			DC	*Washington*
			MA	Bristol, Dukes, Hampden, Hampshire, *Suffolk*, Worcester
			MD	Baltimore County
			NJ	Atlantic, *Essex*, *Hudson*, Ocean, Passaic
			NY	*Bronx*, *Kings*, *Queens*
			PA	Delaware, Philadelphia
			RI	Providence
Affluent noncosmopolitan	$59,158	4.1	CT	Litchfield, Middlesex, Tolland
			MD	Anne Arundel, Calvert, Carroll, Charles, Frederick, Queen Anne's
			NH	Rockingham
			NJ	Gloucester, Sussex, Warren
			PA	Bucks, Chester
			RI	Washington
			VA	Clarke, Fauquier, Spotsylvania

Table 7-1.   County Typology (continued)

	Household income	Percentage foreign born	State	County
Poor noncosmopolitan	$44,509	3.8	CT	New London, Windham
			DE	Kent
			MA	Barnstable, Berkshire, Franklin
			MD	Baltimore City, Cecil, Talbot
			ME	Cumberland, York
			NH	Merrimack, Strafford
			NJ	Cumberland, Salem
			PA	Berks, Cumberland, Dauphin, Lancaster, Lehigh, Northampton, Pike, York
			RI	Kent, Newport
			VA	Culpeper, King George
			WV	Jefferson
Very poor, very noncosmopolitan	$38,447	2.1	MD	Caroline, Kent, Washington
			ME	Androscoggin
			NJ	Cape May
			PA	Carbon, Lackawanna, Lebanon, Luzerne, Perry, Wyoming
			VA	Warren
			WV	Berkeley

Note: Counties in italics have less than 50% owner occupation.

Alexandria, both in Virginia, and New York County have owner occupation rates of 43.4, 40, and 20.1 percent, respectively—much lower than the average for Megalopolis counties, 68.1 percent. In these counties private renting meets the needs of the more mobile, affluent, single-person and nonchild households.

The *poor cosmopolitan* places are located in two areas. First, there are the central cities, such as Washington, Philadelphia, and Providence, and the New York City counties of Bronx, Kings, and Queens. Typical of this subcategory is Queens, where 46.1 percent are foreign born, almost one of every two people, and the median income is $42,439. These are the archetypal immigrant gateways, providing the platform for lower-income immigrants from overseas and newcomers to the city. Private renting dominates in this category of counties. The Bronx has only 19 percent owner occupation; Kings, New York, and Hudson, New Jersey, have only 27.1 percent and 30.7 percent, respectively. Second, there are the industrial counties in New Eng-

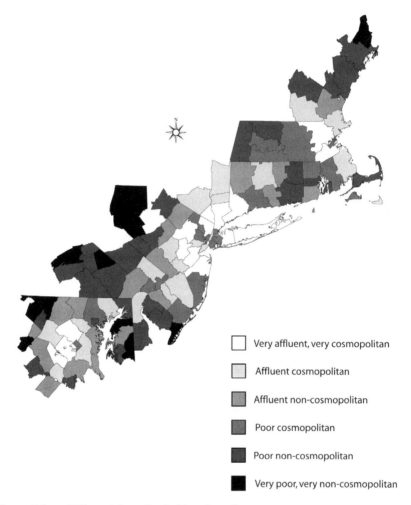

Figure 7-2a.   **Different Counties in Megalopolis**

land and New Jersey, which have incomes below the regional average but some foreign-born population. Worcester, Massachusetts, is typical, with a median income of $47,874 and 7.9 percent foreign born. Located farther from the growth of the major metro areas, these counties have experienced economic decline in the wake of deindustrialization. A Hispanic underclass has sometimes developed against this background of major job loss.

The *affluent noncosmopolitan* counties have a very distinct spatial distribution. They are found on the periphery of the metro areas in areas of more recent suburban growth. This category represents the outermost commut-

WASHINGTON D.C.
REGION INSET

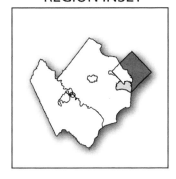

NEW YORK CITY
REGION INSET

☐ Very affluent, very cosmopolitan

▦ Affluent cosmopolitan

▨ Affluent non-cosmopolitan

▩ Poor cosmopolitan

▨ Poor non-cosmopolitan

■ Very poor, very non-cosmopolitan

Figure 7-2b.   Different Counties in Megalopolis

ing edges of the expanding fluid Metropolis. These areas have yet to reach the level of diversity found in other parts of Megalopolis.

The *poor noncosmopolitan* and the *very poor very noncosmopolitan* are primarily counties at the outermost reaches that have been bypassed by economic growth and flows of immigration. They are the rural fringes and declining industrial areas of Megalopolis, sidelined by economic history and geography. There is one urban exception, Baltimore City. Here, the economy has experienced deindustrialization without attracting new producer services, and its population is predominantly low income. Baltimore City is on the margins of the region as much as the counties of Maine. But herein lies an opportunity and possibility. These counties have lower house prices, more land, and cheaper labor. In subsequent waves of private investment, housing construction, and suburban subdivisions, they may become the next scene of intense activity as the fluid metropolis keeps moving outward to cheaper sites and inward, as in the case of Baltimore, to possible sites of gentrification. It is already happening as the expensive Boston housing market pushes some households farther out into Maine and New Hampshire and the overheated Washington housing market makes some people look to Baltimore City as a place for cheaper urban living still within commuting distance to the nation's capital. At the bottom end of the immigrant and income scales, these two categories of counties provide opportunities and possibilities for subsequent waves of investment, commuting, and housing construction and renewal.

SUMMARY

A relatively simple statistical exercise has provided a useful perspective on socioeconomic change in the region. Affluent, cosmopolitan counties are located around the metro areas of Washington, New York City, and Boston. Less affluent cosmopolitan areas are found in urban counties that act as immigrant gateways with low levels of owner-occupied housing, selected suburban counties, and what we may term industrial counties, such as New Haven and Worcester. The poorer, less cosmopolitan places are located on the periphery of the region in the more distant rural and industrial counties as well as in Baltimore City. The two forces of household income differentiation and immigration are like crosscurrents that produce a series of four barrier islands; at the far opposite ends are affluent cosmopolitan and poor, noncosmopolitan counties, and between them the less affluent cosmopolitan and affluent noncosmopolitan. The barrier island metaphor is also fitting when we think of populations moving from one to another. The archetypal immigrant gateway areas are the home base for those who serve the households of the richer cosmopolitan areas. Although this analysis points to the space between the islands, the flows of commuting, shopping, and recreation link them together in complex networks.

The classification indicates a continuum from affluence to poverty and from cosmopolitanism to noncosmopolitanism. And these differences have important implications for county governments. It is no accident that Montgomery County has been running a budget surplus while Baltimore City is in permanent fiscal squeeze. The distinction between rich and poor counties has important implications for the generation and disbursement of county revenue. Similarly, high levels of foreign-born residents affect social service and education. Counties with many immigrants have to make adjustments to a more diverse school population and deal with language issues. The classification, while simple, is profound in terms of the consequences for city and county governments and governance.

CHAPTER EIGHT

SUBURBAN DIFFERENCE

Each year the FBI produces a report on crime. The 2005 report, based on 2004 data, identified Camden, New Jersey, as the most dangerous city in the country, with a homicide rate 10 times the national average and a robbery rate 7 times the national average. The safest place was the Boston suburb of Newton, which had no homicides and the lowest crime rate in the entire nation. Both places are in Megalopolis, revealing that below the level of counties is a complex mosaic of very different places.

The reliance on county-level data provides a focus on political administrative areas with substantial degrees of political autonomy as well as observation units that remain stable over our 50-year period. This focus is limiting, however, failing as it does to pick up the important variation expressed by the more locally based FBI statistics. County data are coarse aggregates that can tell us only so much. For a more nuanced understanding of social change and social difference, it is important to consider data at a finer-grained scale. This chapter undertakes an analysis of urban places.

The primary source of data is the *State of the Cities Data System,* a data set produced by the U.S. Department of Housing and Urban Development

(HUD). This publicly available data set contains census place-level data for a variety of socioeconomic measures. The U.S. Census Bureau defines three types of urban places: census designated places (CDPs), consolidated cities, and incorporated places. CDPs are defined by Census in conjunction with local governments: they are places that are unincorporated with concentrations of population, housing, commercial sites, and a degree of local identity. Consolidated cities and incorporated places are political municipalities with their own local governments that administer services to residents. We identified 2,353 urban places in Megalopolis in 2000.

ANALYSIS OF THE VARIABLES

For each of those 2,353 urban places, 39 variables were selected from the 2000 census (Table 8-1). These variables cover important dimensions of population, income, family structure, education, housing, and employment—variables that commonly appear in both classic and contemporary studies of urban differentiation (Shevky and Bell 1955; Swanstrom et al. 2004).

The resulting data matrix of 39 variables for 2,353 places is large and cumbersome. To simplify the picture, we performed a principal components analysis (PCA), a statistical technique that transforms a large number of variables into a new, smaller set of composite variables, or principal components. This technique acts as both a data reduction method and a process for identifying the most important empirical elements embedded in a data set. PCA has long been an important tool in deciphering the spatial organization of urban places. More recently, it has become an extremely popular technique in market research for classifying residential neighborhoods (Cooper and Schindler 2003). It is ideal for analyzing our large data matrix and highlighting variation among urban places in Megalopolis.

The main outputs of PCA are component loadings and component scores. Component loadings measure the relationship between the original variables and the resulting components, thus allowing an identification of the components. Component scores measure the relationship between the places and the components.

We selected five principal components. Table 8-2 indicates that the five components accounted for 62 percent of the total variance. Component 1 accounted for nearly 29 percent of the total variance, and components 2 and 3 added 10 percent each, for a cumulative total of almost 50 percent.

Table 8-1.   Variables in Principal Components Analysis

Variable category	Variable
Population characteristics	% of population black
	% of population white
	% of population Hispanic
	% of population other race
	% of population foreign born
Income characteristics	% of persons living in poverty
	% of families below 20th U.S. income percentile
	% of families above 80th U.S. income percentile
	Median family income (MFI)
	Ratio of MFI to MFI of MSA
	Median household income
	Ratio of MHI to MHI MSA
Family structure	% of population married with children
	% of single-parent family with children
Educational attainment	% of population did not graduate high school
	% of population high school graduate
	% of population college graduate
Housing characteristics	% of owner-occupied housing units
	% of renter-occupied housing units
	% of vacant housing units
	% of housing units with 3 rooms or fewer
	% of housing units with 4 to 6 rooms
	% of housing units with at least 7 rooms
	% of housing units built before 1939
	% of housing units built between 1940–1949
	% of housing units built between 1950–1969
	% of housing units built between 1970–1989
	% of housing units built after 1990
Employment and occupation	% of labor force in arts, entertainment, recreation, accommodation, and food services industry
	% of labor force in education and health services industry
	% of labor force in manufacturing industry
	% of labor force in finance, insurance, and real-estate industry
	% of labor force in information industry
	% of labor force in professional and scientific industry
	% of labor force in wholesale and retail trade industry
	% of labor force in public administration industry
	% of labor force in services occupations
	% of labor force in management
	% of unemployed persons

Table 8-2. Variance Explained in Principal Components Analysis

Component	Percentage of variance	Cumulative percentage of variance
1	28.61	28.61
2	10.41	39.01
3	10.19	49.14
4	6.50	55.64
5	6.39	62.02

The first three components account for almost half of all variation in the data. Together, the five components "explained" almost two-thirds of the initial variation. In other words, we reduced the number of variables substantially without losing too much information.

The component loadings outlined in Table 8-3 allow us to interpret the meaning of the components. Component scores range from 1 to –1; values closer to 1 indicate a positive correlation, and numbers closer to –1 suggest a negative relationship. For component 1, the key loadings refer to income, education, and employment in managerial occupations. We have termed component 1 "income and education." This finding reinforces previous studies that show that socioeconomic status and education are key factors in the stratification of U.S. society. From Shevky and Bell (1955) to more recent studies, this component has persistently been uncovered as the primary source of urban differentiation in the United States. The persistence of this finding is testimony to the continuing primary importance of class and income in the urban differentiation in advanced capitalist societies. This component distinguishes a continuum between urban places comprising high-income, well-educated professionals and those places with poorer, less-educated residents.

The most important loadings for component 2 are variables that measure black populations, single-parent households, and poor households. These variables allow a relatively easy identification as "the underclass." This component measures places on a scale composed of, on the one hand, white, middle-class families and, on the other hand, black, poor single parents, picking up the polarization between urban places in Megalopolis and the hypersegregation of the poor.

The loadings for component 3 highlight foreign-born people, racial minorities, and renter households. We have termed this component "immigrants and renters," since it distinguishes immigrant, high-rental urban places from home-owning places in Megalopolis. The component reflects the high level of immigration into selected places within the region and the creation of immigrant gateways throughout the region.

Table 8-3.   Component Loadings

Variables	Rotated component loadings				
	1	2	3	4	5
% population black		0.542			0.699
% population white		-0.542			
% population Hispanic			0.711		
% population other race			0.703		
% foreign born			0.881		
% population in poverty		0.684			
% families below 20th income percentile		0.638			
% families above 80th income percentile	0.922				
Median family income (MFI)	0.924				
Ratio of MFI to MFI MSA	0.857				
Median household income (MHI)	0.902				
Ratio of MHI to MHI MSA	0.864				
% married-couple family with children		-0.577			
% single-parent family with children		0.598			
% did not graduate high school		0.581			
% high school graduate	-0.840				
% college graduate	0.900				
% owner-occupied housing unit			-0.529		
% renter-occupied housing unit			0.529		
% housing built between 1940 and 1949				0.770	
% housing built between 1970 and 1989				-0.845	
% housing built after 1990				-0.749	
% workers in public administration					0.819
% workers in services occupations					
% workers in management occupations	0.868				
% population unemployed		0.598			

Note: Rotated using Varimax with Kaiser Normalization in 16 iterations.

The loadings for component 4, which we term "older housing," identify areas with an older housing stock. Emerging from the loadings for component 4 is the dichotomy between the aging, inner-ring suburbs and newer residential developments, often on the outer fringes of metropolitan areas in Megalopolis. Many inner-ring suburbs, particularly in the Megalopolis region, are now more than 50 years old and experiencing decline (Jargowsky 2003; Lucy and Phillips 2000; Puentes and Warren 2006). Inner-ring suburban decline juxtaposed against the growth of the outer suburbs acts as visible evidence of suburban restructuring in Megalopolis.

Component 5 has only two important loadings, black population and public sector employment. We have termed this component "black and government workers" because it identifies places with a copresence of a high percentage of black residents as well as a relatively high percentage of people working in public administration. We suggest that this component highlights the emergence of a black middle class associated with public employment. High component scores are found in the Washington metro area in particular, pinpointing the importance of federal government employment to the creation of a black middle class.

FIVE URBAN CLUSTERS

The components we have identified combine both traditional sources of differentiation such as socioeconomic status with other components more distinctive to our study. As well as the familiar differences across the income and educational attainment scale, there are new source differentiations, including the hypersegregation of the poor, the high levels of immigration into Megalopolis, the decline of selected inner-ring suburbs, and the emergence of a black middle class strongly correlated with government employment. In sum, our results reflect the initial variable selection, echo traditional social area analysis, and identify new processes of social transformation and urban differentiation.

Each urban place in Megalopolis has a score for each of the five components. To identify places of similarity, we conducted a cluster analysis on the component scores for each place in Megalopolis. A "k-means clustering analysis" was performed because it is designed for a large number of observations. We adopted the five-cluster solution because it combined the qualities of ease of interpretation and clearly identifiable clusters. Table 8-4 indicates the distribution of cluster cases. We have given the following names to the five clusters: Middle America, Affluent, Immigrant Gateways, Black Middle Class, and Underclass. Table 8-5 provides statistical comparison of the five clusters. We summarize the dominant features of each cluster in Table 8-6.

Table 8-4. Clusters in Megalopolis

Cluster	Cases	Percentage of total cases	Percentage of total population
Middle America	1,554	66	36
Affluent	266	11	6
Underclass	188	8	16
Immigrant Gateways	229	10	36
Black Middle Class	116	5	5
Total	2,353	100	100

Table 8-5.   Statistical Comparisons of Clusters in Megalopolis

	Affluent	Underclass	Black Middle Class	Immigrant Gateways	Middle America
% population black	3%	44%	29%	11%	5%
% population white	90%	40%	61%	61%	88%
% population Hispanic	3%	11%	4%	17%	4%
% population other race	4%	4%	6%	10%	3%
% foreign born	8%	9%	8%	25%	6%
% population in poverty	5%	19%	6%	9%	7%
% families below 20th percentile of income	8%	30%	9%	14%	14%
% families above 80th percentile of income	41%	12%	31%	28%	21%
Median family income (MFI)	$84,100	$40,215	$68,650	$61,304	$56,689
Ratio of MFI to MFI MSA	134%	67%	102%	93%	94%
Median household income (MHI)	$73,349	$35,363	$61,818	$52,840	$48,864
Ratio of MHI to MHI MSA	142%	72%	109%	95%	98%
% married-couple family with children	83%	49%	70%	73%	75%
% single-parent family with children	17%	51%	29%	27%	25%
% did not graduate high school	10%	29%	12%	19%	18%
% high school graduate	26%	37%	27%	28%	37%
% college graduate	40%	12%	31%	30%	21%
% owner-occupied housing unit	81%	54%	73%	54%	72%
% renter-occupied housing unit	19%	46%	27%	46%	28%
% housing built between 1940 and 1949	8%	14%	3%	9%	10%
% housing built between 1970 and 1989	26%	18%	43%	29%	24%
% housing built after 1990	11%	5%	27%	8%	10%
% workers in management occupations	45%	23%	42%	37%	31%
% workers in public administration	4%	6%	14%	5%	6%
% population unemployed	3%	10%	4%	5%	4%

Note: Table is composed of averages for each of the diagnostic variables identified by the PCA. K-means cluster results.

Middle America is the largest cluster, with 1,554 urban places—66 percent of all places in Megalopolis. The population of Middle America is 35.7 percent of the total population of urban places in this giant urban region. Just over one in three people in Megalopolis live in this type of place, a testimony to the extent and pervasiveness of a mass middle class. The most distinctive feature of the United States and Megalopolis is the large size and importance of the suburban middle class. The 266 Affluent places account for only 6.1 percent of the total population in Megalopolis. And although the Immigrant Gateways number only 229 places, they contain 36.4 per-

Table 8-6.   Summary of Clusters' Dominant Features

	Demographics	Income	Education and employment	Housing	Examples
Affluent places	Mostly white; married parents	Very high income; low poverty	College graduates; management occupations	Newer, large housing stock; high home-ownership rates	Scarsdale, NY; Chevy Chase, MD
Underclass places	Black; Hispanic; single-parent families	High poverty; low income	High school drop-outs	High rental; older housing stock	Camden and Asbury Park, NJ
Black Middle Class places	Mostly black; some single-parent families	Middle income; low poverty	College graduates; high public sector employment	Built after 1970s; high home-owner-ship rates	Bowie and Mitchellville, MD
Immigrant Gateway places	A quarter foreign born; Hispanic and other races high; mostly married couples with children	Low to middle income; some poverty	College graduates; some high school dropouts; varied education levels	High rental; low homeown-ership rates	Hoboken, NJ; Tysons Corner, VA
Middle America places	Mostly white, married fami-lies; "1950s image" of suburbia	Low to middle income; low poverty	High school graduates; some college	Mostly home-owners; post-war bedroom communities	Levittown, NY; Dundalk, MD

cent of the population. The Underclass has 188 places with 16.3 percent of the population, and the Black Middle Class cluster of 116 places contains 5.2 percent of the population.

Middle America places have, on average, a median household income of $56,227, slightly more than the national median household income of $41,994. These places are predominantly white, middle-class suburbs, and the majority of the housing stock is owner occupied. A classic example of Middle America is Levittown, New York, the suburb created by the famous Levitt Company, which built tract housing in both Long Island and Pennsylvania after World War II. In 2000, Levittown had a median household income of $69,923. Almost 90 percent of Levittown residents are white, married, and own their own homes. Almost 90 percent of the housing stock in this suburb was built before 1970, very characteristic of other early post-war suburbs in the United States.

Another example of a Middle America suburb is Dundalk, Maryland, an older, industrial suburb adjacent to Baltimore City. Dundalk was, for almost a hundred years, the home of Bethlehem Steel Corporation until the company filed for bankruptcy in October 2001. It was one of the first planned communities in the nation, built for local steelworkers. In many ways, Dundalk is a prime example of a stable suburb of "average" American families. However, as a traditional steel town, this suburb has witnessed declines in manufacturing employment. The consequences have been increased poverty and declining household incomes. The clustering of Dundalk as a Middle America urban place indicates the wide range of characteristics among places in this cluster. In 2000, the median household income in Dundalk was almost $40,000, much less than the median household income for Levittown residents. The percentage of parents who were married was 61 percent in Dundalk compared with 87 percent in Levittown. In 2000, the homeownership rate in Dundalk was 17 percent less than the rate in Levittown. Dundalk is showing more signs of decline than Levittown.

Places in the Affluent cluster have, on average, a median household income of $73,349, much higher than the median household income of their respective metropolitan area and substantially higher than the national median income of $41,994 in 2000. In these affluent suburbs, 81 percent of the residents own their own homes. These places are overwhelmingly white, and 40 percent of the population have college degrees. Examples of these high-income places are Chevy Chase, Maryland, in the Washington metro area, and Scarsdale, New York.

Chevy Chase is a small, rather exclusive community of fewer than 1,000 households, located northwest of Washington. In 2000, the town was 92 percent white, and 88 percent of the population had college degrees. There were few renters in this affluent community: 95 percent of housing units were owner occupied. The median household income in 2000 was $160,332, two and a half times that of the Washington area and considerably higher than the national median household income of $41,994.

Chevy Chase has a long-established reputation for quiet, understated affluence. The character began to change in the early 2000s with the teardown and replacement of existing homes with very large houses. Land lots are small in the municipality, but the cachet of a Chevy Chase address and the closeness of the community to downtown Washington and employers such as the National Institutes of Health continue to attract the wealthy—and those wanting to display their wealth. Plans for taller houses with large footprints galvanized some residents to propose that the town adopt a six-month building moratorium to stop what they saw as the crass "mansionization" of the built landscape. The town council declared a building moratorium in late 2005. The battle pitched those seeking to maintain the integrity of community designs against those asserting the rights of individual property owners. The struggle, in microcosm, represents the wider tension between community standards and individual rights. The tension is more obvious when both sides tend to be affluent, organized, and politically articulate.

Scarsdale is similarly affluent, although it is an urban place with a much larger and more diverse population than Chevy Chase. In 2000, almost 18,000 people lived in Scarsdale, 82 percent of them white. However, Scarsdale has a rather large Asian population, with almost 4 percent of the population Japanese, 3 percent Chinese, 2 percent Indian, and 2 percent Korean. This urban place had a median household income of $182,792 in 2000, almost four and a half times the median household income of the New York metropolitan area. According to the 2000 census, the population of Scarsdale is highly educated: 80 percent of the people over age 25 are college graduates. Many members of the workforce in Scarsdale are managers and professionals, with 20 percent employed in finance, information, and real estate, and 26 percent employed in the health and educational fields.

The Affluent places in Megalopolis contrast with the poor, Underclass places, where the median household income, $35,363, is 25 percent less than the median household income of their respective metropolitan areas. Residents in the Underclass cluster earn $6,369 less than the national median household income; 29 percent did not graduate high school, 51 percent of families are headed by a single parent, and 30 percent of families were below the 20th percentile of income nationally. Although many central cities in Megalopolis exhibit the pathologies associated with the Underclass cluster, Underclass places are also found well outside central city areas, indicative of a wider spread of poverty than popularly imagined. Although concentrated in central cities, pockets of poverty are located throughout Megalopolis, even in more suburban and semirural areas.

Two telling examples of Underclass places are Asbury Park and Camden, both in New Jersey. Asbury Park, once a thriving seaside resort, has been in decline since the 1960s. With increased prosperity and improved air travel, the lure of this once-bustling resort waned. After a race riot in the 1960s, white flight ensued. The population in 2000 was more than 60 percent black and 15 percent Hispanic, and the poverty rate was 30 percent. The median household income in Asbury Park was $23,081 in 2000, almost two-thirds less than the median household income of its metropolitan area and almost $19,000 less than the national median. In 2000, 70 percent of families were single-parent families, and 80 percent of housing units were rental properties.

Camden, another example of an Underclass urban place, developed in the shadow of Philadelphia (Kirp et al. 1995). In the early 20th century it experienced tremendous industrial growth. The gramophone was invented in the Nipper Building, home of the Victor Talking Machine Company, later the Radio Corporation of America (RCA). At its peak in the 1950s, RCA employed more than 20,000 people spread over 50 buildings in the city. By the 1960s, decline had set in as manufacturing employment disappeared. The city lost jobs and population. Retail establishments and the middle class have moved out to suburban New Jersey. From a total of 125,000 in 1950, this city now has a population of less than 80,000 people. Almost half of the population is black, and 40 percent is Hispanic. Largely a place of minorities, it has witnessed increased poverty and income declines in recent decades. The poverty rate increased from 20 percent in 1970 to 35 percent in 2000, and the median household income was $23,421 in 2000, less than half the median household income of the metropolitan area. Camden exhibits many of the social pathologies associated with concentrated poverty, including the dubious distinction of being at the top of the FBI's list of most dangerous cities. Almost half the population did not graduate from high school, 68 percent of parents are single, and more than half the people do not own their homes. And as in other cities in distress, there are plans for revitalization. Camden is focusing on a waterfront development similar to Baltimore's Inner Harbor. The aim is to build up-market apartments and the usual elements of the standard urban spectacular—shops, museums, aquariums, high-rise office buildings—along the shared waterfront with Philadelphia.

Megalopolis also comprises Immigrant Gateways. On average, these places have populations that are almost 25 percent foreign born. Immigrant Gateways are also places where 46 percent of residents rent homes. These areas are otherwise very similar to Middle America places, in that income levels are similar to metropolitan area incomes, and three-quarters of all parents in these places are married. The population is slightly more educated than the population of Middle America, with 30 percent college graduates. The proliferation of Immigrant Gateways, particularly in the New York and Washington regions, reflects the new waves of immigration. Two examples are Hoboken, New Jersey, and Tysons Corner, Virginia, in the Washington area.

Hoboken is a densely populated city on the west side of the Hudson River, across from Manhattan. This area has been a hub for immigrants to the United States for decades. It was a destination for many Italians and Irish immigrants living in the New York region. Other ethnic groups followed, most notably the Puerto Ricans in the 1960s. According to the 2000 census, 15 percent of the people of Hoboken are foreign born, and more than 20 percent are Hispanic. More than three-quarters of families living in Hoboken rent homes. Rental properties are the mainstay of housing in this area, similar to many other areas close to New York City.

Tysons Corner is the archetypal edge city: located off the Washington Beltway, it is home to Tysons Corner Center, a massive retail complex that includes 230 stores, 3,400 hotel rooms, and 25 million square feet of office space. The population of Tysons Corner is 18,540, with almost 35 percent foreign born, and 70 percent have four-year university degrees. The foreign-born population is composed largely of Hispanics and Asians. Tysons Corner is a good example of an immigrant suburban settlement that contains different racial groups and immigrant streams with differing skill sets.

On average, Black Middle Class places have a population that is 29 percent black. The median household income is $61,818, slightly more than the median household income in their respective metropolitan areas, and $20,000 more than the national median household income; 73 percent of housing in Black Middle Class places is owner occupied, and 70 percent of parents in these areas are married. Almost 31 percent of the population graduated from college, and 14 percent of the workforce is employed by local, state, or federal government. This cluster is one of the most distinctive features emerging from our research. Few other studies of this nature have identified such a distinctive cluster of places that can be legitimately identified as black middle class. We should note that this category does not identify all black middle-class areas. The nature of the grouping program links places with shared characteristics across all the components; areas of black affluence where more people work in the private sector are thus not included in this category. This category does not exhaust all affluent black places in Megalopolis. Two examples of Black Middle Class places are Bowie and Mitchellville, both in Maryland in the Washington area.

Bowie is the largest municipality in Prince George's County and the fourth-largest city in Maryland. It has a population of more than 50,000 people, 30 percent of whom are black. The median household income in Bowie is $76,778, almost 25 percent higher than the median household income in the Washington area and 80 percent higher than the national median household income; 85 percent of housing units are owner occupied, and 80 percent of parents are married. Almost 18 percent of workers

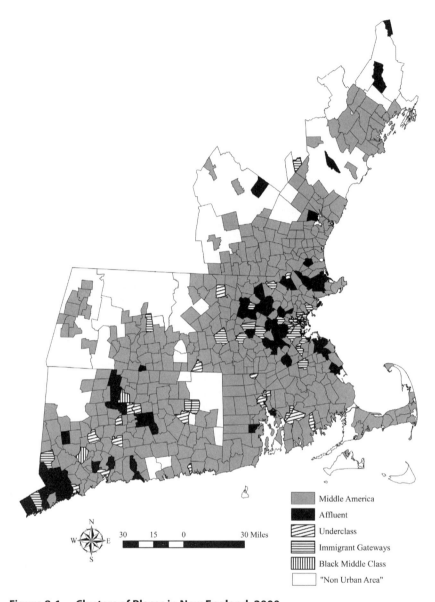

Figure 8-1.   Clusters of Places in New England, 2000

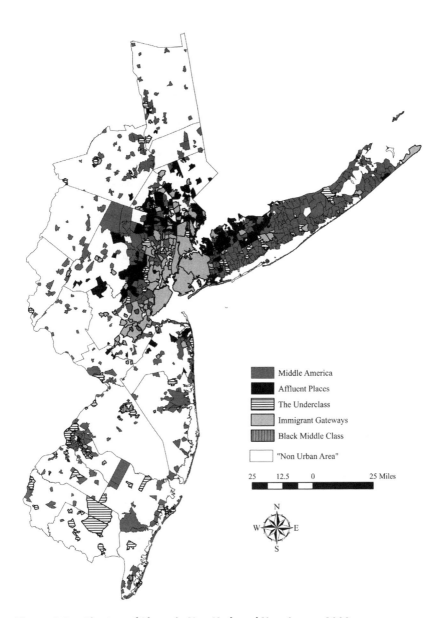

Figure 8-2.   Clusters of Places in New York and New Jersey, 2000

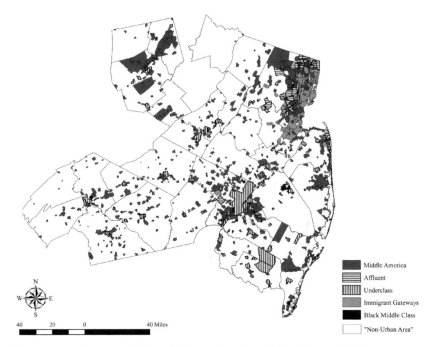

Figure 8-3.   Clusters of Places in Pennsylvania and New Jersey, 2000

are employed in the public sector. It is a typical middle-class place, where steady government employment offers stability to many families.

Mitchellville has a population that is 78 percent black. This suburb of Washington has a median household income of $84,687, which is 37 percent higher than the median household income of the metropolitan area and double the national median. More than 73 percent of parents are married in this highly stable suburb. Almost a quarter of the workforce is employed in the public sector, and 94 percent of the housing units in Mitchellville are owner occupied.

The details of the analysis would be lost if only one map was used to represent the entire region. We will thus consider the spatial distribution of these clusters though a discussion of maps of the four major metro areas. Figure 8-1 shows the cluster distribution in New England. The map is dominated by Middle America places. There is a concentration of Affluent places strung along Route 128 around Boston and in the southwestern corner of Connecticut, where the outer suburbs of New York City—also Affluent places—cross the state line. Inner Boston encompasses a cluster of Immigrant Gateways. There are pockets of Underclass places scattered throughout the area showing up local areas of poverty and deprivation.

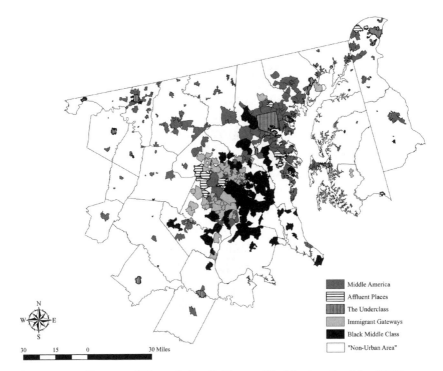

Legend:
- Middle America
- Affluent Places
- The Underclass
- Immigrant Gateways
- Black Middle Class
- "Non-Urban Area"

Figure 8-4.   Clusters of Places in the Baltimore-Washington Corridor, 2000

Figure 8-2 shows places in New York and New Jersey. New York City stands out as a significant Immigrant Gateway. Many of the Middle America suburbs stretch down the spine of Long Island, running parallel with the "gold coast" of Affluent places in the north of the island. These Affluent places create a band of wealth around New York City. There are also numerous pockets of poverty highlighted by the Underclass places, primarily in the deindustrialized sections of New Jersey.

In Figure 8-3 the Underclass places cluster around Philadelphia and Camden but are also widespread throughout the region, again indicating a more spatially dispersed pattern of urban poverty than popularly imagined.

One of the most interesting features of Figure 8-4 is the obvious presence of Black Middle Class places in the Baltimore-Washington corridor, reflecting the contribution of government employment to the rise in black social status. Black Middle Class places form a wedge to the northwest of Baltimore and an arc around Washington from northeast to south. The rest of the suburbs around Baltimore are predominantly Middle America, and in Washington, Immigrant Gateways predominant, with a sector of wealth running northwest from the city.

FOUR TRENDS

Over the past 50 years, Megalopolis evolved into a complex region of diverse urban places. Our analysis of census places using principal components analysis highlights four distinct trends. First, economic power is the largest explanatory factor for variation among urban places in Megalopolis. Wealth and education, or their lack, are paramount in the creation of the urban social landscape. Second, the identification of an underclass suggests that there is increasing polarization between not only central city and suburban cores, but also within suburban areas. Third, because the Megalopolis region has experienced the return of a mass immigration not witnessed in more than a century, Immigrant Gateways can be identified in both central areas and suburban places. Fourth, there is some evidence of the decline of first or inner-ring suburbs. Here, the housing stock has aged along with the local residents, and many of these places are experiencing socioeconomic decline. Inner suburban decline juxtaposed against the growth of the outer suburbs supplies the visible evidence of suburban restructuring in Megalopolis.

Fifty years have passed since Gottmann's seminal study. Megalopolis remains a significant center for the nation's population and economic activity. At the same time, the forces of urban decentralization have made the region a more fully suburbanized agglomeration. We reveal a complex socioeconomic pattern of a vast urban area structured by class, education, housing tenure, housing age, and race and ethnicity. The cluster analysis identifies four distinct new urban places—Affluent, Underclass, Black Middle Class, and Immigrant Gateways—in addition to the places of Middle America that loomed so large in the Gottmann study.

CHAPTER NINE

URBAN NEIGHBORHOODS

Although the census place data provide a finer-grained grid than the county-level data, they are still aggregated. The entire city of Baltimore, for example, is identified in our cluster grouping classification as Underclass while the whole of Washington, D.C., is classified as Immigrant Gateway. Both are large cities with substantial neighborhood variations that transcend the singular identity of this place data analysis. There is a scale below census places, the census tract, that provides an even finer-grained net to identify different places within Megalopolis. These tracts are the basic collection unit used by the U.S. Census Bureau. They are small, with populations ranging from 1,200 to 6,000, and are drawn so that they are the nearest statistical unit to what is commonly referred to as local neighborhood. In this chapter I will use census tracts to provide closeups of places within the large cities and illuminate the more important sources of urban change and stability. I have chosen 10 census tracts, 3 each in Boston and Washington and 4 in Baltimore, that provide a rich contrast in urban neighborhoods across Megalopolis. The simple statistics provided in Table 9-1 reveal very different urban worlds.

THE POLARIZED CITY

One of the most dramatic changes across Megalopolis in the past 50 years is that mass suburbanization has siphoned off the middle-income white families from the city. In more recent years there also has been a suburbanization of the black middle class. In the wake of this movement, cities have become very polarized, as increasingly only the very poor and the very affluent remain.

In their study of household income distribution in U.S. cities, Berube and Tiffany (2005) show that the largest cities in the nation house a disproportionate share of low-income households. Using their typology of the 100 largest cities in the country, we note that cities in Megalopolis fall into three main categories:

- *Stressed*, where there are twice as many households in the bottom two quintiles of income distribution as in the top two; cities in this group include Baltimore, Philadelphia, and Newark.
- *Low-moderate*, where there are more households in the poorer categories than in the richer categories, although not as marked as in the stressed category; examples are Jersey City, Boston, and New York.
- *Divided*, where there is a U-shaped income pattern with very few middle-income households; cities in this category include Washington and Yonkers, New York. In Washington, for example, the median family income range by census tract extends from a high of $345,117 to a dismal low of $17,592.

The selective nature of suburbanization has left behind the affluent and the poor. Deep racial cleavages overlay these wide income differences.

THE AFFLUENT CITY

Affluent areas exist even in the poorest of the big cities. The aggregate data for Baltimore, for example, paint a picture of poverty and decline. And in the Berube and Tiffany classification it ranks as one of the most stressed of cities. However, the tract level can identify well-to-do areas like Roland Park (Table 9-1). This area was first developed by the Roland Park Company in 1891 and was a garden suburb by the very early 20th century. Frederick Law Olmstead was hired to lay out the western portion. He used the natural to-

Table 9-1.   Census Tract Data

Area	Census tract	Household median income	Percentage black	Percentage foreign born
Boston		$39,629	5.3	26.0
Beacon Hill	201	$81,804	0.7	11.2
South Boston	608	$41,976	0.4	12.3
Roxbury	818	$25,111	76.6	13.6
Washington		$40,127	61.0	13.0
Cleveland Park	13	$130,186	6.1	19.0
Navy Yard	200	$23,942	97.0	0.0
Columbia Heights	28	$46,220	32.0	54.0
Baltimore		$30,078	64.0	9.8
East Baltimore	0704	$13,971	98.0	0.7
Federal Hill	2403	$53,917	7.2	6.1
Roland Park	2714	$67,107	5.2	7.3
Pimlico	2717	$31,223	91.9	12.0

pography to pleasing effect. Houses were built to a uniformly high standard with stylistic variations, predominantly Queen Anne shingle with smatterings of Georgian and Regency Revival and the latest Arts and Crafts. The designs created diversity within a shared aesthetic. Extensive communal plantings gave the area a pronounced coherence. A country club, first established in 1898, also cemented the sense of community. Edward Bouton and William Edmund initially developed Roland Park as a utopian community with a diverse and differentially priced housing stock. Restrictive covenants were imposed to maintain the quality and integrity of the development. However, the area soon became an elite residential area, a cachet that it retains to this day. In a majority black city, census tract 2714 in Roland Park is 89 percent white and 75 percent have a bachelor's degree or higher. The median household income is $67,107, which is almost double the city average.

The other two cities also have areas that have maintained their exclusivity. Consider Cleveland Park in Washington and Beacon Hill in Boston: they remain areas of stable exclusivity, overwhelmingly white. Like Roland Park, these are planned developments from the late 19th and early 20th centuries with an architectural coherence and high quality of design. They are traditionally elite areas, long associated with the city's rich and powerful. The areas retain their appeal for the wealthy and connected and have resisted the roiling urban changes that have affected less powerful groups and less affluent neighborhoods.

THE POOR CITY

At the opposite extreme from Beacon Hill, Cleveland Park, and Roland Park are areas such as East Baltimore and the southeast quadrant of Washington, neighborhoods of intense poverty where the poor live in hypersegregation. In census tract 0704 in East Baltimore, for example, 98 percent of the residents are black and the median household income is only $13,971. The per capita income, $8,306, is low even by Baltimore standards. Almost one in two families lives below the poverty line, and those above it are struggling. Only one in two people who can work is formally employed. This is one of the least fortunate areas of Megalopolis, a place largely unaffected by rising incomes and increased affluence.

Census tract 200 lies within Southeast Washington. Geographically opposite Northwest, where Cleveland Park is located, it is also demographically opposite: overwhelmingly black and poor. The median household income is $23,942, virtually all —97 percent—residents are black, and in a sure sign of isolation from the mainstream, no foreign-born residents were identified.

In a recent study Jargowsky and Yang (2006) suggest that the number of underclass census tracts dramatically declined in the 1990s across the nation's cities, from 1,148 in 1990 to 775 in 2000. They draw upon previous work that identifies underclass areas using the four indicators of unemployed men, teenaged school dropouts, female-headed households with children, and households on public assistance. They suggest that the decline of the underclass tracts is due to a combination of factors, including economic growth that lifted wages for low-income workers and provided more employment opportunities for the unemployed, the decline of crack addiction, federal income assistance, and the demolition of high-rise public housing concentrated in inner-city areas. Their findings are reinforced by the work of Kingsley and Pettit (2006) of the Urban Institute, who note a drop in concentrated poverty for the 100 largest metro areas in the United States, from 31 percent in 1990 to 26 percent in 2000. Although this may be true at the national level, there are still underclass tracts in places like East Baltimore and Southeast Washington that provide a stubborn counterexample to improvement and progress.

Poor areas are also found in the richer cities. Census tract 818 in the Roxbury area of Boston is poor and black and provides a telling counterpoint to the white affluence of Beacon Hill. Three of every four people are black and the median household income, $25,111, is less than a third of the median income in Beacon Hill. In the large cities of Megalopolis there are very rich and very poor neighborhoods, people in the same city but inhabiting very different worlds, one of mobility and affluence, and choice, the other of restriction, stasis, and poverty.

THE CITY OF CHANGE

We can identify areas that have changed. Pimlico in Baltimore, for example, was traditionally a Jewish middle-class area. Over the years, the Jews moved north, although the Baltimore Hebrew University remains as a testament to the former character of the neighborhood. The 2000 snapshot of census tract 2717 reveals a predominantly black area. Pimlico, like the rest of the city, has become majority black.

In other cases gentrification occurs. In selected inner-city neighborhoods there has been an in-movement of higher-income households. The Federal Hill area in Baltimore is very close to the Inner Harbor. The century-old dwellings have been refurbished as middle- and upper-income households move into the downtown location. For those without children and with downtown employment, Federal Hill provides a convenient location and attractive urban experience. Census tract 2403 is now 88 percent white, with 93 percent owner occupation and a median household income much higher than the city average.

In some cases inner-city change is fueled by the influx of the foreign born. The Columbia Heights section of Northwest Washington has become a Hispanic neighborhood. Now more than half the people in census tract 28 were born overseas, and 51 percent are Hispanic. In central city census tracts throughout Megalopolis, decades of population decline reverse as the newcomers move in from overseas.

Among the changes there are also areas of stability; census tract 608 in South Boston continues to be an overwhelmingly white, blue-collar part of the city. However, South Boston stands out in a city that is becoming more gentrified. In Boston the bottom two quintiles of income distribution made up 54.8 percent of the city population in 1970 but only 49.61 percent in 1999. The corresponding figures for the top two quintiles were 25.6 percent and 31.9 percent. In the less economically buoyant cities of Megalopolis, the trend went the other way. Using Berube and Tiffany's classification, both Baltimore and Philadelphia moved from low-moderate to stressed between 1979 and 1999 while Boston moved from stressed to low-moderate.

In the central cities of Megalopolis, the dominant themes have been polarization between rich and poor areas, the decline of areas of concentrated poverty, the gentrification of selected areas, and the influx of the foreign born in some neighborhoods. There are areas of stability, including the long-established affluent areas and the entrenched, very poor areas. However, it is change that has been the most dramatic feature. The processes of polarization, gentrification, segregation, and immigration mark the central city experience of Megalopolis.

CHAPTER TEN

MEGALOPOLIS
AS A GLOBALIZING CITY REGION

I n this chapter I argue that the forces of increasing globalization have made Megalopolis the capital city region of the world: a pivotal point of command, control, and narration in the contemporary world.

At the beginning of his 1961 book, Gottmann portrays the region as the Main Street of the nation. Later, in Chapter 3, he describes it as the continent's economic hinge. He saw the region primarily in terms of national importance and to a lesser extent of continental importance, but the forces of globalization then were so relatively weak that global prominence was only embryonic and thus scarcely visible to Gottmann. Today, the region can be identified as one of the dominant globalizing city regions in the world.

DEFINING GLOBALIZATION

We have been living in a truly global world for more than 500 years. Columbus's landing in the Caribbean began a global exchange between the eastern and western hemispheres that created a truly global world. People, animals, viruses, goods, and ideas began moving between geographically separate continents. It is more accurate to think of globalization as a series of pulses that connect and disconnect different places in different ways. Between 1880 and 1914, for example, there was a significant upswing of globalization trends as international standards and organizations were established, including the Olympic Games and various sports federations, as well as postal unions and international time zone agreements. Another pulse was felt when a new world order was established immediately after World War II, with the creation of the United Nations, International Monetary Fund, World Bank, and General Agreement on Tariffs and Trade, the precursor to the World Trade Organization. These institutions and frameworks, in association with a neoliberal political agenda, laid the basis for a still more powerful pulse of globalization.

Thomas Friedman (2005) writes of the flattening of the globe. In *The World Is Flat* he describes the processes of outsourcing, offshoring, and information sharing that have created a more level playing field for economic collaboration and competition across the world. Economic globalization, in other words, has created a more fully integrated global economy. However, in the flat world, small differences become magnified. Small differences in wage rates between different parts of the world assume huge significance, and accessibility, once measured in days and months, is now calibrated with reference to hours, minutes, and even seconds. On closer inspection, the flattening of the world is only partial. Significant valleys and peaks are still evident: although India and China are more fully part of the global economy, some other economies have become dislodged from the wealth of the global economy. And even within individual countries there are enormous variations. Global cities in particular are places of concentrated global accessibility, different from places just a few hours away.

So far we have been using the general term *globalization*. We can begin to see some of the complexity by making a distinction between economic, political, and cultural globalization. Economic globalization involves the rapid flows of capital around the world, the lengthening production chains of goods and services that cross borders, and the increasing interconnectivity between the economies of different countries. There has been a global shift in manufacturing and a consequent decline of the male working class in Europe and North America and the creation of a new female working class in South and East Asia. National territories have lost their homogeneity now that islands of global connectivity differ increasingly sharply from the rest of the national economy. Economic globalization is creating profound differences between economic sectors and job categories, and between parts of the country and the city.

Political globalization is evident in trade, aid, security, and environmental issues. The world is now organized along more global systems of regulation, monitoring, and control. This is not to argue for the death of the nation-state. In fact, distinct elements of the nation-state are reinforced by globalization because some parts, especially central banking systems and trade departments, play a pivotal role in managing the global-national nexus. We can identify both an embrace of this globalization and a resistance to it. On the one hand there are progressive global discourses of environmentalism, human rights, social justice, and economic equity. World public opinion created and maintained by global media coverage often has been an important lens in which national dictatorships and local regimes are viewed. Cosmopolitanism is now a more active agent in global politics and domestic power relations. On the other hand, there are also resistances and reaction. When the present is ever changing and the future is uncertain, the past becomes a place of security. The rise of fundamentalism in the strands of the world's largest religions—Hindu, Islamic, Christian, and Jewish—is a promised return to fixed, unchanging categories. Fundamentalism and cosmopolitanism are the two interconnected poles of the social reactions to globalization.

Cultural globalization is the degree to which similar cultural forms are found around the world. This has led some to account for the process of cultural homogenization, often portrayed as a form of Americanization. Although U.S. popular cultural forms are disseminating much more wildly and deeply around the world—more people speak a form of English, eat at McDonalds, and watch Hollywood movies than ever before—this has not led to an upsurge in pro-American sentiment. If anything, quite the reverse. There is a subtle difference between the production of cultural forms and their consumption across the world. The consumption of culture is not a passive process of indoctrination but a more active process of incorporation and creative readings. Despite the similarity of cultural forms, their consumption varies across the world as new and old, indigenous and exotic cultural forms are innovatively combined. The process of cultural globalization creates as much difference as similarity. New cultural identities emerge around hybrid forms as well as around invented traditions that are resistances to perceived cultural imperialism.

The current round of globalization forges difference and divergence around the world. Minor differences in wage rates are exacerbated in a truly global economy; new hybrid identities materialize as culture is pried loose from its traditional locational constraints. Difference and divergence, change and recombination are the new order of the day. Globalization is restructuring traditional forms of economic, political, and cultural difference and similarity.

A flat world is not necessarily a homogeneous world. Similar goods and images are used and incorporated in different ways in different parts of the world. Different locales have different ensembles of the same images and goods. Despite shared languages of consumption and exchange, regional variations are still important. Think of the way that multinational corporations now have strategies to "brand" global commodities for different markets. Globalization has created complex patterns of hybrids rather than a common standard of homogeneity. Similar goods are consumed differently around the world. The English language has been creolized into different dialects, and more people now use several languages and variants of the same language depending on the context of communication. More groups are combining local and national identities with a cosmopolitan identity to produce a rich mosaic rather than one all-encompassing global identity.

Dominant narratives have a way of crowding out alternatives. The dominant globalization narrative emphasizes an integrating world economy, a homogenizing global culture, and a coherent global polity. It may be instructive to end this section by noting the possibility of alternative discourses that focus on globalization as a process that generates fractured economies, splintering cultures, and resurgent nation-states.

GLOBALIZING CITY REGIONS

An important topic of current urban research is the exploration of the links between globalization and cities. Recent research emphasizes the identification of a global network of world cities through the colocation of advanced producer services (Taylor 2004), infrastructure such as airline connections (Taylor et al. 2006), and Internet links (Townsend 2001). Although this work is important in identifying the global urban networks, it is less useful as a way of identifying processes of globalization *within* urban regions. Work on the city-globalization nexus is skewed toward external links, with comparatively less attention devoted to the internal processes of change or to the connections between external links and internal restructuring.

The theorization of the links between the city and globalization has also been based on the experience of very few cities. Los Angeles, for example, has been identified as the unique site of new forms of postmodernity and its pattern of development put forth as a model for other cities (Dear 2001;

Scott and Soja 1996). The building of metatheories precariously balanced on a narrow range of cities, or in this example just one city, is unlikely to lead to a nuanced understanding of the variation and complexity of urban change around the world.

We will use the term *globalizing city region* (GCR) to refer to large urban agglomerations that are vital nodes in global networks as well as sites of complex sociospatial articulations (Scott 2001; Short 2004). These city regions are motors of the global economy as well as sites of new forms of urban living and spatial organization.

Richard Florida and Steven Pedigo have calculated the gross domestic product of metro regions around the world. For 2005, the four major centers of Megalopolis rank among the top: New York is first with $170 billion, Philadelphia fifth with $90.6 billion, Washington sixth with $79.4 billion, and Boston-Providence seventh with $76.4 billion (Florida 2006).

Megalopolis is the world's most important GCR where the different processes of globalization are readily apparent. In terms of economic globalization, two themes can be identified. First, the region has seen the global shift in manufacturing employment unfold across its industrial landscape. The decline in manufacturing employment in the region directly relates to the flattening of the world's manufacturing production. Jobs previously done in New York, New Jersey, Boston, and Baltimore are now done in cities in Vietnam and China. The relentless drive to cut costs prompted the movement of manufacturing employment from higher-wage regions like Megalopolis to GCRs in China. More recently, there has also been a shift in service employment as back-office enterprises including billing, design, and data management move to places like Bangalore, where wage rates are lower. The metal-bashing jobs have gone from Megalopolis, and the routine data-management jobs are not far behind. Left behind are the jobs that cannot be outsourced (yet), such as gardening, construction, and food service, as well as the jobs in the sectors where Megalopolis has a distinct advantage, the advanced producer services.

The Globalization and World Cities (GAWC) team working at Loughborough University in England has generated the best comparative data on advanced producer services. In 2000 they collected data on 100 firms in six key areas—accountancy, advertising, banking, insurance, law, and management consultancy—with offices in 15 or more cities. The resultant data set allows a global network connectivity ranking of 315 cities. London and New York are the core hubs of the global urban network. The top six are London, New York, Hong Kong, Paris, Tokyo, and Singapore; they also retained their positions from 2000 to 2004 (Taylor and Aranya 2006) and are the principal connecting points of the global economy. New York along with London plays a lead role at the very top of the global urban hierarchy. New York dominates other U.S. cities (Table 10-1); it is the U.S. global city. In their analysis of U.S. cities in the global network, Taylor and Lang (2005) find that U.S. cities are less globally connected than cities in Europe and Pacific Asia. U.S. cities are more strongly linked to other U.S. cities than to other cities around the world.

The data used by GAWC discriminate the different cities of Megalopolis: in their rankings New York is clearly preeminent, followed by Washington, Boston, Philadelphia, and then Baltimore. The central spine of global connectivity in Megalopolis decisively links Boston, New York, and Washington. The most globally linked city to both Boston and New York is Washington. Consider airline connections: Table 10-2 shows the airline connections of major carriers within Megalopolis on just one day, February 20, 2006. On that day there were 69 flights between Boston and New York and 129 between New York and Washington. These are major hubs in their own right, so there is little hub-and-spoke movement that can inflate the connections between major and minor airports. The data reveal a high level of connectivity indicative of a closely linked urban system. Combining the GAWC data for the five big cities would make Megalopolis the center of the global urban network.

The region is also an important destination in the global movement of people. Benton-Short et al. (2005) have constructed a global urban hierarchy of immigration. For 150 cities around the world, they created an index based on the percentage of foreign-born residents in the city, the total number of immigrant residents, the percentage of immigrants not from a neighboring country, and where no one country provided more than 25 percent of the immigrants. They identified a three-stage hierarchy. At the apex of their 10-city alpha category was New York. Washington was in the middle of the 10-city beta category, and in the 35-city gamma category was Boston.

Table 10-1.   Global Connectivity of Cities in Megalopolis

City	Global network connectivity (max=1)	Rank
New York	0.976	1
Washington	0.418	7
Boston	0.351	8
Philadelphia	0.268	13
Baltimore	0.178	24
Hartford	0.142	32
Wilmington	0.059	40

Source: Taylor and Lang (2005).

Table 10-2.   Air Connectivity within Megalopolis

		Departures				
		Boston	New York	Philadelphia	Baltimore	Washington
	Boston	—	69	19	13	86
	New York	70	—	10	11	129
Arrivals	Philadelphia	21	9	—	7	12
	Baltimore	17	14	6	—	*
	Washington	42	64	12	*	—

*Too close for flights via major carriers.

These three Megalopolis cities were first, sixth, and fourth in their respective categories. Together the three cities constitute the single most globally connected city region in the world for immigration. The global position of the 3 top-ranked cities in Megalopolis is shown in Table 10-3.

For over a century Megalopolis has been an important destination for foreign immigration. In her careful analysis of historical data from 1900 to 2000, Audrey Singer (2005) identifies three types of immigrant gateways within Megalopolis:

- *Continuous immigrant gateways*, which had above-average foreign-born immigration in every decade of the 20th century, include Bergen-Passaic, Boston, Jersey City, Middlesex-Somerset-Hunterdon, Nassau-Suffolk, New York, and Newark.
- *Former gateways*, where foreign-born immigration was above average from 1900 to 1930 but below average thereafter, include Baltimore and Philadelphia.
- *Emerging gateways*, which had very low amounts of foreign-born immigration until 1970, followed by higher-than-average immigration from overseas. Washington is a prime example.

Although the region as a whole has been a continuous immigrant gateway, the development of former and emerging gateways reflects the changing economic fortunes of specific urban economies.

Good indicators exist for urban global network connectivity for producer services and immigrant flows, but we have very few data on indicators of political globalization. Nevertheless, it is obvious that Washington is the capital of the world's remaining superpower. The second half of the 20th century witnessed the rise of the United States to global prominence and since 1989 to the position of the world's hyperpower. Although the data are difficult to assemble, averaging out the various estimates puts U.S. military spending somewhere between 35 and 45 percent of the total military spending in the entire world. The United States easily outspends the combined military expenditure of the next 10 countries. There are few instances in recent history where there has been such asymmetry in global military power. Washington is the imperial center, home to the military-industrial-scientific complex that undergirds U.S. global power and dominance. The Washington metro area has grown in lockstep with the rising global dominance of the United States. The city has developed from a sleepy southern town into a major metropolis, the capital embodiment of the world's hyperpower. The city also houses the headquarters of important institutions of global economic governance and control: just a few city blocks from the White House sit the headquarters of the International Monetary Fund and the World Bank. And throughout the city are some of the most important clusters of nongovernment international agencies in the world as well as constellations of embassies, missions, and other foreign representation. Most countries reserve their largest overseas representation for Washington.

At the other end of the central spine of Megalopolis, New York houses not only one of the world's most important stock markets and banking establishments but also the permanent headquarters of the United Nations. Within Megalopolis is a concentration of global economic and political power that is second to none. The region is a primary hub of the global urban network and the epicenter of economic and political globalization.

In 1790 the fledgling republic of the United States decided upon the location of a national capital. It was a compromise decision. Alexander Hamilton wanted New York, but his critics saw the city as too dominated by bankers and merchants. The city of trade would corrupt the republic. Thomas Jefferson and others in the Virginia planter class wanted a southern agrarian location, away from the power of the bankers and the clamor of the abolitionists. At a dinner in June 1790, attended by Hamilton, Jefferson, and James Madison, a deal was struck. Philadelphia would be the temporary location before the capital was established on the banks of the Potomac. In return Hamilton got support for his financial plan for the assumption of state debts by the federal government.

On July 19, 1790, the House approved the Residence Act, which made a 10-square-mile district on the Potomac the permanent capital. For almost 180 years the divisions between political and economic interests, North and South, agrarian and urban persisted in the separation of New York and Washington. The capital long remained a small, provincial southern town. Even by the middle of the 19th century George Combe could describe it as a "large straggling village reared in a drained swamp"—or as John F. Kennedy characterized it almost a century later, a city of "southern efficiency

Table 10-3.   Global Urban Immigration Rank of Cities in Megalopolis

City	Global Urban Immigration Rank
New York	1
Washington	16
Boston	24

Source: Benton-Short et al. (2005).

and northern charm." The cosmopolitan commercial hustle of New York seemed distant. Jefferson with his distrust of the market and the city would have been pleased. But more than 200 years after the deal was struck to appease the competing interests of the early republic, the rift is narrowing. Washington is now more cosmopolitan, and politics and business intermingle just as they do in New York. The space-time differences between the two cities have shrunk; telephones and Internet, trains and cars and planes, as well as shared political ventures and joint commercial endeavors connect the two cities in myriad intricate relationships. As the region of Megalopolis coheres and coalesces, the two cities meld and mingle. Hamilton, a believer in a strong federal government and abolition (unlike the slave-owning Jefferson) would be pleased. The separation laid down by the Founders has been overcome by the viscosity of the liquid metropolis. In Megalopolis, North and South, political and economic, polis and market are, at last, combined in a single globalizing city region.

CHAPTER ELEVEN

REGIONAL ISSUES

Τhe issues facing this large, liquid metropolis are many and varied. Although each city, county, and municipality faces unique problems associated with its particular location, some issues run across these boundaries. In this chapter I want to consider four: sprawl, transportation, affordable housing, and the metropolitan fragmentation of government.

SPRAWL

By sprawl I mean the liquid suburban expansion that has spread out across the region in a low-density, largely unplanned fashion. Galster et al. (2001) show that urban areas in Megalopolis have some of the lowest amounts of sprawl, with New York, Philadelphia, and Boston having the lowest figures among all urban areas in the United States. Atlanta and Miami, in contrast, have some of the highest.

Recent, detailed work on sprawl reveals a complex picture across the country. Lang (2003a) shows that sprawl takes different forms. In the wet Sunbelt, sprawl is typically low in density, whereas in the dry Sunbelt, because of aridity, public lands, and slope constraints, sprawl is of higher density. In Megalopolis it takes the form of a very low-density fringe in association with dense urban cores.

Sprawl is the sum of myriad small and large residential and commercial developments that spread an urban penumbra across the landscape. The term *sprawl* often has a negative connotation. James Howard Kunstler (1993) is just one of many critics who use the contemporary suburban landscape to marshal a critique of U.S. society. For Kunstler, the landscape of strip developments, shopping malls, dead city centers, and congested suburbs embodies the overwhelming power of the profit motive and lack of aesthetic sensitivity. Sprawl is a text that tells a story of environmental degradation, social fracturing, and loss of community. He writes,

> Born in 1948, I have lived my entire life in America's high imperial moment. During this epoch of stupendous wealth and power, we have managed to ruin our greatest cities, throw away our small towns, and impose over the countryside a joyless junk habitat which we can no longer support. Indulging in a fetish of commercialized individualism, we did away with our public realm, and with nothing left but our private life in our private homes and private car, we wonder what happened to the spirit of community. We created a landscape of scary places and became a nation of scary people. (Kunstler 1993, 273)

Robert Putnam (2000) also argues that suburban sprawl is an important cause of civic unraveling. There are also some defenders of sprawl. In his book *Sprawl: A Compact History*, Robert Breugmann (2005) provides a vigorous defense of low-density scattered urban development at the edge of cities. His book is an extended argument that sprawl has always been a part of urban development, and that it reflects the desires of the consumers. The criticisms of sprawl, he believes, reflect the class bias of intellectual elites.

Sprawl provides some benefits. It gives middle-income households access to a wide range of safe, affordable homes in tight housing markets. A wide scatter of workplaces and retail and commercial development spreads economic opportunities throughout the metropolis. But there are costs to sprawl in addition to the ones already mentioned. The first is the reliance on oil-based, private transport. Sprawl is a form of development that is too diffuse to support public transport or easy walking. The heavy and in some cases total reliance on private autos imposes a heavy environmental price in terms of air pollution and the increasing dedication of space for roads and parking. The reliance of a built form precariously balanced on costly fossil fuel raises issues of long-term sustainability.

There are ecological costs. Urban sprawl creates more paved surfaces. When 10 to 15 percent of the land surface is paved, increased runoff and chemical pollutants reduce water quality; at 15 to 20 percent, oxygen levels in streams fall markedly; and at 25 percent, many organisms die. Volstad et al. (2003) conducted just one of the many studies that document the local impairment of streams with the increase of urban land use in Megalopolis.

The loss of green space, defined as nonurban land use, is particularly acute in areas of rapid growth. A study of the Washington metro area showed that the 3,000-square-mile region lost 50 percent of its green space between 1986 and 2000. In this short period the proportion of developed land increased from 12.2 to 17.8 percent. The data in the report suggest that 28 to 43 square miles of green space disappear every single day (Metropolitan Washington Council of Governments and the National Park Service 2004). One developer responded to the report with the observation that long-established building regulations that focus on low densities force the building of sprawl (Williamson 2004).

As sprawl continues outward, more land is needed. The rapid growth in Montgomery County, Maryland, just north of Washington, has meant increased traffic. A new intercounty connector, first proposed in the 1970s, is now scheduled for construction. The 18-mile, $2.4 billion road linking Interstates 270 and 95 will affect streams, wetlands, and other sensitive ecological areas in its path. Pressure from community and environmental groups has resulted in the construction of bridges over the wetland and floodplains but the impacts will still be large. And in the wake of the road will come more sprawl. The solutions to sprawl often create the conditions for greater sprawl.

There are a variety of responses to the problems of sprawl. We can characterize them as resistance, smart growth, and New Urbanism. Resistance occurs at all scales. It occurs especially in growth areas with more affluent households. In the high-growth areas, rapid increase in traffic, overcrowded schools, and higher local property taxes can all stimulate local resistance. In Howard County in Maryland, for example, where population grew 32 percent from 1990 to 2000 and another 7.6 percent to 266,738 in 2004, some residents began to resist the latest round of development proposals (Spivack 2005). The powerful development-homebuilding lobby marshals its forces against such resistance. When residents in Howard County signed a petition to call a referendum to challenge rezoning proposals, a group of landowners sued the council to cancel the referendum.

Resistance is particularly strong when the local residents are wealthy and organized. Mark Singer (2003) describes a struggle in a wealthy Connecticut town as one between the haves and the haves. The town of Norfolk is a place of old money, and obvious displays of affluence are frowned upon. Almost 80 percent of the town's 30,000 acres is designated as forest, agriculture, or park. An area of 780 acres known as Yale Farms came on the market in 1998. A plan to develop a luxury golf course and a hundred homes, each on four acres, generated intense resistance from groups that called themselves the Canaan Conservation Coalition and the Coalition for Sound Growth. The fight, according to Singer, has given people "a chance to affirm their shared values." Behind the debates about loss of green space and loss of community was fear of change and a distaste for the incoming *nouveaux riche*.

Resistance takes many forms, from "not here," and "not this here" to "not this here now." The success of the resistance depends upon the wealth, organizational skill, and effective links to political power of the pressure groups. But the battle is uphill and in many cases unsuccessful. The resistance movement, though successful in a few areas, has clearly failed to halt the spread of sprawl across the region.

One planning response to sprawl is "smart growth," which stresses mixed land uses and compact building designs that create high densities with lower environmental impact. Smart growth has emerged as a strategy to deal with the constant pull of development toward greenfield sites on the city's edge; it focuses on existing developments to utilize their infrastructures and to preserve open space and farmland. It is a framework for municipalities facing heavy development pressure and looking for principles and policies to halt the abandonment of urban infrastructure and costly rebuilding in greenfield sites.

In 1996, the Smart Growth Network enunciated its principles: mix land uses, design more compact buildings, construct walkable communities, create a sense of place, preserve open space, direct development toward existing communities, provide a variety of transport choices, encourage community involvement in development decisions, and make fair, predictable, and cost-effective decisions. If implemented, smart growth may halt the seemingly relentless expansion of the suburban fringe into open spaces.

In 1997 Maryland established a set of smart growth policies with three main goals: to target state resources to areas where infrastructure was already in place; to preserve farmland and natural resources; and to slow public investment in building infrastructure that promoted sprawl. A set of priority areas were identified for state funding of transportation, water, and sewer systems. In effect, the policy guided higher-density development in areas already served by public infrastructure. Areas such as Silver Spring, Maryland, with good bus and metro links saw higher-density developments as planners sought to direct developments to already built-up areas. The Maryland smart growth initiative, led by Governor Parris Glendenning, became a model for other states. The statewide scheme was abandoned in 2002, with the election of Governor Robert Ehrlich, but at the county level a variety of smart growth strategies continue. In Montgomery County, for example, planning proposals include the encouragement of high-density mixed land use, the use of infill developments, and plans for more development at bus, metro, and rail stations and the transformation of roads into boulevards (Lewis 2005).

Another response to sprawl is New Urbanism, which is less a public policy for land-use management and more a design guide for builders and developers. It emphasizes revitalizing old urban centers; creating mixed-use centers with residences located close to commercial and office buildings; constructing walkable, high-density, low-rise residential areas that are socially diverse communities; minimizing the speed of autos through urban areas, and in general making neighborhoods more attractive to walking and casual social interaction. The design blueprint has only just started to be turned into buildings on the ground.

Across Megalopolis sprawl continues to cover the landscape. There is successful resistance in certain areas and a few examples of smart growth and New Urbanism. But the dominant trend is low-density suburban development beyond the edges of the central cities. The continually centrifugal forces of suburban growth are creating a dispersing liquid metropolis.

TRANSPORTATION

The main transportation issue facing this giant urban region is congestion. The level of traffic is on the verge of overwhelming the infrastructure. In the Washington metro area, to take just one example, between 4:30 and 5:30 P.M. on weekdays, a quarter of all freeways are very congested. The Texas Transportation Institute publishes regular measurements of travel times and congestion costs for all metro regions in the United States. According to the 2005 report the Washington metro area has the 3rd-worst traffic congestion in the country, as measured by annual delay in hours; New York is 13th, Baltimore is 17th, and Philadelphia is 27th (http://tti.tamu.

edu/documents/mobility_report_2005.pdf). When congestion costs, which include the costs of delay and extra fuel, are factored in, New York is the 2nd most costly, at $6,770 million, Washington is 7th, at $2,463 million, and Philadelphia is 10th, with $1,334 million. An indication of the intense congestion in Megalopolis is available from the American Community Survey of commuting times in 2002. Table 11-1 shows the times for cities and counties in the region with the longest commuting times. The cities and counties of Megalopolis have the longest times in the whole country.

The road networks are so overloaded at key points that minor accidents can lead to major traffic snarls and long delays. The increased traffic is also damaging the infrastructure because as more cars and heavier trucks pound the roads, the need for repair and maintenance expenditures increases.

The spine of the regional road network is I-95, which runs north-south through the region. The traffic has increased on this route in the past decade at a rate of 4.4 percent more cars per year. There is also more commercial traffic because just-in-time production systems reduce stock inventory and stores must be resupplied on a more frequent basis.

Because of costs, community resistance, and the realization that building more roads often just generates more traffic, the emphasis of public policy has shifted from increasing the supply of roads toward the more efficient management of traffic. New solutions call for spreading truck traffic from the ports to reduce congestion, greater use of toll roads, raising existing tolls, using congestion pricing to encourage off-peak driving, metering freeway ramps, coordinating signals for connecting arterial roads, and introducing "E-Z pass" systems that let drivers prepay tolls. The policy shift is too recent for an effective evaluation. However, the congestion costs imposed on both business and individuals within Megalopolis remain a serious matter. What of the other regional transport alternatives?

The region is just large enough to have airline connections between the cities within Megalopolis. Boston, New York, and Washington are far enough away to make air travel justifiable. Frequent shuttle flights link cities in Megalopolis. However, since September 11, 2001, the reduction in flights, increase in costs, and heightened security measures are all making relatively short flights less attractive.

If this were any other megalopolitan region in the world, the obvious transport solution would be high-speed rail. Megalopolis is one of the few urban regions in the United States suitable for rail. Relatively high densities and existing infrastructure all make rail travel a viable alternative to car or air travel. There are already commuter rail links within the major city regions (Table 11-2). Attempts at greater regional rail integration have not

Table 11-1.   Average Daily Commuting Times in Cities and Counties in Megalopolis, 2002

	Minutes	National rank
City		
New York City	38.4	1
Philadelphia	30.3	3
Baltimore	29.7	5
Washington	29.4	6
Boston	28.2	10
Newark	27.6	11
County		
Bronx, NY	41.8	1
Queens, NY	41.4	2
Richmond, NY	41.2	3
Kings, NY	39.9	4
Prince William, VA	35.5	5
Prince George's, MD	34.6	6
Nassau, NY	34.1	7
Monmouth, NJ	32.4	11
Suffolk, NY	32.0	12
Westchester, NY	32.0	12
Plymouth, MA	31.7	14
Rockland, NY	31.6	15
Montgomery, MD	30.9	16
Orange, NY	30.2	22
Somerset, NJ	30.0	23
Dutchess, NY	30.0	23
Ocean, NJ	29.8	26
Hudson, NJ	29.7	27
Middlesex, NJ	29.7	27
New York, NY	29.4	30
Anne Arundel, MD	29.0	35
Howard, MD	28.8	37
Fairfax, VA	28.6	38
Rockingham, NH	28.5	39
Bergen, NJ	28.5	39

Source: U.S. Census, American Community Survey, http://www.census.gov/acs/www/index.html (accessed October 2, 2006).

been successful, however. The rail passenger network in Megalopolis is run by Amtrak, a "quango" (quasi-autonomous national government organization) created in 1971 as a way for private rail companies to off-load their federal mandate to provide passenger transportation. The precipitous decline in train travel had made the railroads unprofitable. Amtrak was given responsibility for a 22,000-mile rail network without ownership of most of

Table 11-2.   Passenger Rail Traffic in Megalopolis, 2005

City (Station)	Passengers (thousands)	National rank
New York City (Penn)	8,497	1
Philadelphia (30th Street)	3,742	2
Washington (Union)	3,734	3
Newark (Penn)	1,214	6
Baltimore (Penn)	980	7
Boston (South)	971	8

Note: Total passenger numbers include boarding and alightings.
Source: Amtrak.

the track and a severely declining market. In 2005, it earned approximately $1.89 billion in revenue and incurred approximately $2.94 billion in expenses. Amtrak is a perennial target of cuts by Congress.

The most successful market for Amtrak is Megalopolis, where more than 1,700 trains operate over some part of the Washington-Boston route each day. Megalopolis is served by three systems, Acela Express, Metroliner, and the more locally based Regional System. The high-speed Acela Express is the most obvious vehicle for the tighter regional integration. With speeds up to 150 mph, the trains can theoretically link New York with both Boston and Washington in less than three hours. In reality the system has been hampered by problems. New trains were ordered in 1996, but cost constraints led to the selection of the lowest bid, a new design from a Franco-Canadian company, rather than modification to an existing design. At the design stage, numerous changes were made, and federal safety standards mandated a much heavier train than the European equivalents. The result was a very heavy train that suffered from cracked brakes. The service has been disrupted three times since its inaugural run in 1998, the most serious in 2005, when 20 trains were taken out of service. Even with these problems, Acela Express generated revenue of $300 million in 2005. A more reliable high-speed rail system would integrate Megalopolis even more. There are other benefits to encouraging rail traffic in Megalopolis: it reduces the environmental impacts of roads and airlines, since rail travel consumes less energy per capita and generates less pollution than cars or jets. Whether the Megalopolis corridor could be profitable if separated from Amtrak, perhaps in public private organizational form, is a point for discussion. Rail systems like roads and airlines need some measure of government subsidization.

AFFORDABLE HOUSING

In 2006 the median family in Fairfax County, Virginia would have to spend 54 percent of its income to afford the county's median-priced house. In 2001, they would have needed to spend 26 percent. Housing affordability has emerged as a major issue in Megalopolis. There are growing problems of housing for low- and middle-income households in the overheated housing markets of Megalopolis.

The increase in house prices in Megalopolis creates real problems of housing affordability. As prices rise, households have to divert an increasing part of their income to pay rising housing costs. In Frederick County, Maryland, for example, the percentage of housing units affordable to median-income families declined from 42.4 percent in 2000 to only 16.5 percent in 2004 (Kunkle 2006). Residents of Megalopolis confront a paradox: where there are jobs, there are few affordable houses, and where there are affordable houses, there are often few jobs. In some parts of the region, municipalities have responded to the problem of housing affordability in creative ways. Montgomery County, Maryland, introduced a setaside policy. In larger developments, 12 percent of new units were set aside at affordable prices, with a 10-year rule so that housing will remain in the affordable price range for some time. Between 1973 and 2000, more than 11,000 units were set aside. In other parts of the region, especially in the Virginia counties, developers often resist the setaside initiatives and fight them in court. Even more radical solutions include new forms of public housing, such as third-sector housing involving housing cooperatives and housing associations.

Encouraging owner occupation is the government's main and often only housing policy. The extension of owner occupation to lower and lower income groups is not without its problems. Large down payments, high interest rates, and an inability to afford maintenance costs and property taxes often make owner occupation difficult for low-income households. The lower the income, the greater the difficulties. The number of homeowners now spending more than 50 percent of their income on housing rose by 27 percent between 1997 and 2001 (U.S. Department of Housing and Urban Development 2005). A study by Patrick Simmons (2005) points to the rising affordability problem in selected metro areas in Megalopolis from 1990 to 2000. He shows the increase in households with "severe burdens," defined as housing costs that exceed 50 percent of income (Table 11-3).

There is a link between housing affordability and sprawl. Households respond to the growing housing-income gap by moving to less expensive

Table 11-3.   Housing Affordability in Cities of Megalopolis

Area	Percentage of households with severe housing cost burdens	
	1990	2000
United States	6.1	7.7
Baltimore	6.9	11.2
Boston	9.9	10.9
New York City	11.0	15.3
Philadelphia	8.4	11.3
Washington	7.5	10.2

Source: Adapted from Simmons (2005).

homes in the urban fringes, thereby lengthening their commutes to work. This rise in commuting means more traffic congestion, an increase in commuting time, communities left more vulnerable as lower-income but essential service workers such as police, teachers, firefighters, and health care workers have to live farther out, and business growth is sometimes stifled because of difficulties in recruiting local labor. In some cases workers can leverage a tight job market into higher wages, but the housing squeeze is often toughest for the lower-income service workers.

The issue of affordability is highlighted most acutely in growth areas. In fast-growing Arlington County, Virginia, the number of rental units affordable to lower-income groups declined substantially from 2000 to 2005. According to the Arlington County Housing Division, in 2000 there were 60,608 rental units that were available to those earning 80 percent or less of the median household income. By 2005 this figure had dropped to 35,360. The figures for those earning 60 percent or less of the median household income were even more dramatic, dropping from 32,681 in 2000 to 12,688 in 2005. Municipalities in many growth areas have shied away from rent controls or even limitations on rent control increases. Arlington tried to use planning gain measures to solve the affordability crisis, allowing developers to build at higher densities with more stories if they included affordable units, but the developers successfully fought the plan in the courts.

The housing affordability issue will only increase in Megalopolis as more people cram into the growth points of the region. It is particularly acute for low-income and middle-income working families who increasingly have to spend more of their income on housing, commute longer distances, or accept substandard housing. Setasides, rent control, and the encouragement of third-sector housing are possible policy solutions that require careful analysis and some test implementation.

METROPOLITAN FRAGMENTATION

The typical city in Megalopolis is a balkanized arrangement of numerous municipal governments. The degree of fragmentation varies by state. In Maryland and Virginia, for example, school districts are county wide rather than local. Thus Fairfax County in Virginia has just over one million residents and a unified school system that is, with 239 schools, 22,000 staff, 164,000 students, and a $2.1 billion annual budget, the 12th largest in the nation. In New York and New Jersey, in contrast, school districts are more local. Thus Bergen County, New Jersey, with a population similar to Fairfax, has 79 school districts. The more fragmented the districts, the greater the opportunity for inefficiencies and marked disparities in educational attainment.

The large number of local government units in Megalopolis is, in itself, not a problem. There are some—public choice theorists being the most vocal—who would argue that this is a healthy state of affairs. A large number of municipalities in a city region allows residents to choose from a variety of tax loads, school districts, and forms of government. When households can vote with their feet, governments have to be more sensitive to citizens' demands and preferences. The fragmented city can be the city of choice that allows different forms of municipal government to be tried and tested. Not all households have the luxury of such choice. The lower-income households have a restricted choice, and low-income minorities have least choice. There is an important equity issue in opening up the suburbs to low-income households effectively trapped in the central city.

There are other arguments in favor of multiple jurisdictions. Small municipalities are closer to the needs of individual citizens, more accessible, more responsive. They allow ordinary residents and citizens to be engaged. These are convincing arguments for the *status quo* that cannot be dismissed easily. However, there are also problems associated with this fragmentation. We can consider two.

The first is a central city–suburban fiscal disparity. Central cities, especially those with shrinking populations, have an eroded tax base and lower-income population, whereas the suburbs have an expanded tax base and a relatively affluent population. Cities have relied on the property tax as a source of revenue. With declining population and the departure of businesses and higher-income households, the tax base shrinks while the concentration of poorer people places greater demand on services, such as police, welfare, and social services. The older cities also have an aging infrastructure that is expensive to maintain and replace. Moreover, the reduction of intergovernmental aid and the rise of unfunded mandates place extra pressure on struggling cities (Judd and Swanstrom 2006).

Central cities have to deal with the politics of economic decline while many suburbs contend with managing growth. While central cities may witness a downward spiral of shrinking tax base leading to poor services that cause more people to leave, thus shriveling the tax base even further, the growing suburban communities may experience a benign cycle of new residents generating more tax revenue, thus allowing better services, thus attracting even more people. This creates a tremendous inequity in municipal funding, a problem that is exacerbated by the decline of federal funding for many social programs. Municipal fragmentation, which separates out poor cities from affluent suburbs, reinforces the inequalities in U.S. society.

A second related problem is public education. In the United States, the federal government has a very limited role in providing funding and resources to public schools. School funding is dominated by state and municipal sources. States provide on average 50 percent of total school budgets, local districts around 45 percent, based on local property taxes, but the federal government contributes only 5 percent. At the school district level, disparities in wealth feed directly into educational standards and performance.

Jonathan Kozol's (1991, 2000, 2005) work provides the most sustained analysis of differences in educational spending. In Megalopolis affluent suburban districts regularly spend almost double per student compared with inner-city schools. This disparity translates to marked differences in the amount and quality of teachers, facilities, and resources that lead to different levels of educational attainment, which in turn is an important predictor of future income levels. There are exceptions, however. Washington has among the highest per capita spending on students but one of the lowest levels of educational attainment. Concentrated and extreme poverty and a poorly run school district make even this high-expenditure school district a lackluster performer in the standard educational testing of students. For many already-affluent households, public education may provide an escalator to affluence, but for most low-income households trapped in poor school districts, public education fails their children. This is dramatically revealed when we consider attainment on standardized tests. In 2002 the best high schools in New Jersey had a 100 percent pass rate for 11th-grade students in reading, math, and writing tests. The worst school, in contrast, had passing figures of only 17.3 percent for reading, 31.4 percent in math, and 21.6 percent in writing. The best schools were in a wealthy suburban district. The worst was in cash-strapped Newark.

Metropolitan reform, involving a reorganization of municipal government to reflect metropolitan realities, was a significant feature of social policy debates in the 1960s and early 1970s. Daniel Patrick Moynihan (1969), for example, could note that part of the ineffectiveness of urban government in responding to problems derives from the fragmented and obsolescent structure of urban government itself. Since then, notions of national urban policy and metropolitan reform have largely faded from view. There are exceptions. David Rusk (1999, 2003) promotes metropolitan reform. In *Cities without Suburbs,* he argues that the lack of metropolitan reform condemns central cities to limited futures, promotes segregation, and reinforces income disparities between city and suburb. In another book, *Inside Game Outside Game*, he points to policy solutions, including regional land-use planning, metropolitan-wide public housing programs, and mandated city-regional revenue-sharing programs.

Metropolitan government occurs to varying degree in Miami and Portland, Oregon, and city-county consolidation has occurred in Nashville, Jacksonville, and Indianapolis. It is unlikely, however, that the annexation of suburbs into a regional government is a serious contender for implementation in the cities of Megalopolis (Norris 2001; Savitch and Vogel 2004). Suburban resistance is too strong. Although Megalopolis is a functional urban region, it is split by various state boundaries and crisscrossed by local and municipal divisions that tend to exacerbate differences and make regional planning and effective metropolitan government a rare event.

CHAPTER TWELVE

MEGALOPOLIS AND THE FUTURE

W hen Gottmann's *Megalopolis* was published in book form in 1961, he emphasized a modern, industrial city region with defined centers and edges. In the intervening years, the region has become more postmodern, more postindustrial, decentralized, and edgeless. Gottmann's Megalopolis was a manufacturing hub of the national economy, with substantial populations in its central cities, relatively few foreign-born residents, and marked racial and ethnic segregation. The most significant changes include the relative shift of population from the central cities to the suburban counties, the loss of manufacturing jobs especially in the central cities, the growth of services, and the increase in the foreign-born population in both selected central cities and a few suburban counties. Despite all these changes, racial segregation remains a stubborn fact of life in the nation's largest urban region.

The changes have wider cultural implications. In Chapter 2 I drew upon the writings of Zygmunt Bauman. Let me do the same in this final chapter. Bauman (1992) writes of a postmodern condition marked by a loss of certainty about conduct, the unpredictability of change, a lack of centeredness, and the decline of grand narratives. The recent evolution of Megalopolis partly explains this shift. As rapid changes restructure our cities, as more of our lives take place in a decentralized metropolis, as city centers decline, as we follow space-time paths through the metropolis seemingly disconnected from our fellow citizens, and as our truly public spaces are highly segmented, then the oppressive and unsettling sense of continual change is made very real, the loss of grand narratives is made palpable, and the lack of center to social life is made visible. The postmodern condition thrives in Megalopolis.

Megalopolis has grown in population since 1950. Within this general trend there has been a profound redistribution from the central cities to the suburbs that has shifted economic activity and metropolitan vitality toward the metropolitan periphery.

The single most important redistribution of population was from dense cities to thinly spread suburbs. Public policies intensified the pull of the suburbs by encouraging highways and a building boom of single-family dwellings on peripheral greenfield sites. Developers and builders profited enormously, and so did the homeowners whose mortgages were guaranteed by the federal government and whose interest payments were tax deductible.

There were also pushes making the central city a place to leave. Urban renewal schemes in the 1950s and early 1960s demolished many inner-city neighborhoods under slum clearance and highway building programs. Destruction in the name of progress and improvement ripped the heart out of many cities. Perceptions of rising crime, failing schools, and racial divisions all helped push people out. White flight occurred as middle-class whites in particular moved to the suburbs. The move to the suburbs was not only made easy, for many it was also made inevitable. Once in motion, the trek to the suburbs acquired its own self-fulfilling momentum. As more families moved out of the central cities, the tax base of urban school districts shriveled, reducing educational spending, which in turn led to declining schools, forcing out even more families.

A defense of suburbia is possible. It can provide safe, affordable homes, high levels of mobility, and relatively good access to a wide range of goods and services. But the costs are also real: extensive appropriation of rural land and greenfield sites, constant traveling, and a disconnect between residents of central city and the suburb. In this built environment, a heavy reliance on private autos produces more roads, more traffic, higher gasoline consumption, and longer commuting times.

As employment and retail disperse, complex commuting patterns arise. On top of the daily ebb and flow of traffic into and out of city centers—the daily tidal movement of metropolitan United States—there are also more complex flows between distant residences and employment centers. The densities are too low to support mass transit systems, and the result is more auto traffic. Throughout Megalopolis, mounting levels of commuting and traffic generate severe congestion. One solution is to build more roads, and in the short term this can reduce the pressure as well as provide locations for new patterns of growth. Part of the explosive growth in the Washington metro area has been north from the city, along the corridors of Interstates 95 and 270. A new intercounty connector is planned consisting of a six-lane, 18-mile toll road that would link the two interstates just north of Washington. But more roads also generate more traffic, and so an upward spiral occurs: more traffic leading to more roads generating more traffic.

More people in Megalopolis now live in suburban counties rather than central cities, which apart from New York City have lost significant population. The region has changed from a big-city population to a much more fully suburbanized agglomeration. Although the central cities have lost population, new areas of population growth, especially in the Maryland and Virginia counties surrounding Washington, have emerged. This southern growth of Megalopolis is a local consequence of the rise of the military-industrial-scientific complex. The population and economic growth of the Washington metropolitan area of Megalopolis reflects the growth of the federal government and the postwar rise of the United States to a global power.

The more detailed analysis of the 2000 census place data allowed us to identify finer-grained differences within the region and evidence of growing polarization between affluent places on the one hand and underclass places on the other. The principal components analysis also detected the emergence of immigrant gateways and the development of black middle-class suburbs.

The postindustrial shift from manufacturing to services is particularly evident in Megalopolis. There has been a marked deindustrialization in central cities. The large cities, however, continue to attract producer services. This economic change has profound consequences for blue-collar workers, especially those in the central city who have seen their job opportunities disappear and their bargaining position in the labor market weaken. For those trapped in the central city, the suburbanization of jobs has been disadvantageous. Manufacturing job loss has been dramatic especially in the central cities, while the producer services sector has emerged as economically important.

Megalopolis has become more multiracial. Over the 40-year period from 1960 to 2000, whites and Asians especially have become more suburban. Segregation by race remains a significant element in the social geography of Megalopolis. This segregation is not innocent of wider implications in terms of access to jobs, quality of schooling, and the ability of political jurisdictions to respond fiscally to social issues and problems.

The changes have taken place against the backdrop of metropolitan fragmentation of local government. The big cities have lost their tax base while suburban counties have the task of managing growth. The story of the central cities has been dominated by a growing fiscal crisis as they cope with the outmigration of taxpaying citizens and business enterprises and with the continuing need to entice people and investment back to the city. Increased suburbanization has also led to a more pronounced social segmentation. More people live in separated suburbs.

Megalopolis still serves as an ideal research laboratory. The eastern seaboard of the United States remains one of the most highly urbanized areas in the world. We have analyzed broad-scale population and economic trends, identified principal sources of urban social variation, and created a typology of clusters of urban places to identify the internal processes of socioeconomic change in a globalizing city region.

The fluidity of Megalopolis suggests that any spatial demarcation will always be provisional, not permanently confining. Let me end with brief snapshots of counties and neighborhoods on the edge that soon will become a more formal and functional part of Megalopolis.

THE NEW SUBURBAN FRONTIER

The southernmost edge of Megalopolis stretches out into the Virginia countryside. Beyond Spotsylvania and King George's County lies Caroline County (Figure 12-1). It is situated between Richmond and Washington and thus subject to suburban expansion from both the north and the south. Households in search of cheaper housing are moving to the county from both Richmond and Washington. Interstate 95 is the commuting backbone of the county, linking the new developments to job centers in the larger cities. Caroline County is one of the sandwich counties between the formal edge of Megalopolis and an existing metro area outside Megalopolis. The county is experiencing pressure from both ends. Until recently, the county was so far from the major urban centers in the region that it

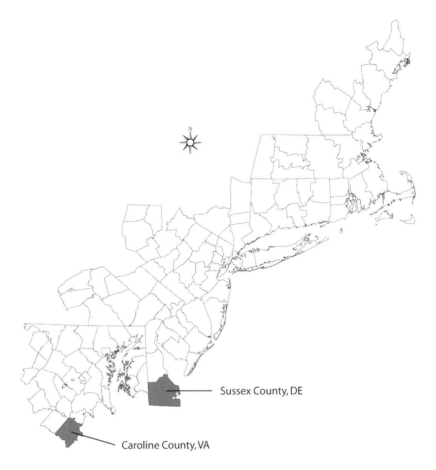

Sussex County, DE

Caroline County, VA

Figure 12-1.   Counties on the Edge

remained predominantly rural and unpopulated, with few new housing developments of any size. But as housing markets heat up in the bigger cities, households are more willing to make longer commutes. McCrummen (2006) documents the case of the Ferrigan family, who moved their home into Caroline Country an extra 20 minutes south in commuting time from their previous home in Fredericksburg. Lori Ferrigan now commutes all the way into Alexandria, Virginia. The Graves family moved into Caroline County from Prince George's County to buy a bigger house and find better schools. As builders respond to the demand and more people make similar decisions, the county's population is growing dramatically. In 2005 it was still only 25,563, yet that was a 5.6 percent increase from the year before, 15.5 percent from 2000, and more than 104 percent since 1950. Caroline is now one of the fastest-growing counties in the country, a traditionally rural county with increasing pockets of new suburban developments, such as the Village at Ladysmith, half-finished and partially constructed, where the Ferrigans purchased a house for $340,000 in 2005. The new housing developments are isolated pockets of suburbia in predominantly rural settings, but as house prices increase in the metro areas, as house builders respond to present and future demand, and as acceptable commute times lengthen, then by the 2010 census Caroline County will be more fully integrated into Megalopolis. The liquid metropolis flows ever outward.

SUBURBS BY THE SEA

In Delaware, Megalopolis formally ends at Kent County. The next county south is Sussex (Figure 12-1). There are two distinct geographies to this county: an agricultural interior dominated by poultry farms and intensive cultivation, and a long, sandy coastline that has attracted tourists for generations. In recent years, the proximity to Baltimore, Washington, and Wilmington has generated growth pressures. The construction of a bridge across the Chesapeake made the county that much more accessible to residents of the Washington metro area. Prior to the bridge's construction, the Delmarva Peninsula (so-called because it contains territory of Delaware, Maryland, and in the extreme south, Virginia) was reachable from Washington only by ferry or a long circuitous land route. The bridge's completion on April 15, 1964, made the area more accessible and opened it up to metropolitan pressure. A parallel crossing to cope with the greater traffic was begun in 1995 and completed in 1999.

Development pressure has taken two main forms. First, there has been an infilling of the coastal settlements as more condos are constructed and vacation homes built. There has been a steady expansion of the coastal settlements with the prime beachfront sites commanding the greatest prices. The small, modest vacation homes of the 1950s and 1960s are being torn down and replaced with year-round monster homes on the dunes. Second, there are large planned developments just inland from the prime coastal sites. Typical are the 1,400-dwelling Peninsula on Indian River Bay, the 1,500-dwelling Isaac's Glen in Milton, and the 2,500-dwelling Plantation Lakes, just outside Millsboro. Gated communities, luxury homes encircling exclusive golf clubs, and up-market retirement complexes are transforming this once-quiet seasonal place into the latest development frontier of

Megalopolis. The county's population has grown from a modest 61,336 in 1950 to 113,229 in 1990 and to 172,216 in 2004. In 15 years the population has grown 52 percent. Kirstin Downey (2005) argues that the sleepy nature of the county makes it unprepared for the development onslaught. Sussex County has no experience of large-scale development and so did not ask developers to shoulder some of the burden that the growing population imposes on government services.

Sussex County may not make the formal definition of Megalopolis because it is, at present, too far for everyday mass commuting. However, the county is linked to Megalopolis as more second homes, retirement communities, and vacation homes are constructed to meet the demand of the wealthier residents of southern Megalopolis. The county is slowly but surely being pulled into the outer reaches of Megalopolis.

FILLING IN THE HOLES

There are also areas being reclaimed at the heart of Megalopolis cities—areas such as Shaw, an approximately 20-block neighborhood in the middle of Washington bounded by Florida Avenue, 15th Street, and M Street. It has long been home to African Americans. Many former slaves who moved to the capital during the Civil War established camps in the area. Throughout the first half of the 20th century it was home to a vibrant, mixed-income black community. Blacks built and patronized local banks, stores, and theaters because they were severely restricted in their housing choices and shopping opportunities elsewhere in the city. The area was the center of Washington's equivalent to New York's Harlem Renaissance. A Supreme Court ruling in 1948 lifted restrictive covenants, and gradually middle-class blacks began to move to other areas; lower-income residents, some pushed out by urban renewal schemes, moved into the neighborhood. In 1960, 92 percent of the 31,901 residents were black. A mixed-income black area was turning into a poor black area. In the 1969 riots that followed the assassination of Martin Luther King, Jr., business premises were torched. Rapid decline set in. The crack epidemic of the 1980s brought violence and addiction. The area deteriorated further; it became seedy and rundown, unaffected by the rising incomes experienced elsewhere in the urban region. As the black experience polarized into an increasingly affluent middle class and an impoverished low-income group, Shaw housed the latter, not the former. By 1980 the population had declined to 18,198. The early 1990s saw a renewal. A Metro subway station opened, Howard University/Shaw, in 1991. The area was now better linked to the wider city, and its central location began to attract development interest. A new convention center opened in 2003 just south of the neighborhood. Property values began to increase, and expensive condos were constructed. A building that opened in 2004 charged as much as $3,000 a month for a one-bedroom apartment. The area was changing. The population of 16,609 in 2000 was more evenly split, with 56 percent black and 44 percent white.

Shaw is located in a zone of major change in Washington. To the east are the predominantly black, poor areas of the city. To the west is the predominantly white, more affluent part of the city. The area is in the middle of an economically polarized city that has a pronounced U-shaped income distribution pattern overlain by attendant racial cleavages. Polarization has been increasing. Over the past 20 years, while the top fifth income group saw an increase from $87,300 to $157,700 (81 percent), the bottom fifth's income barely shifted from $12,300 to $12,700 (3 percent) (Bernstein et al. 2006). Many of the new jobs in the city are held by suburban residents, and much of the affluence has bypassed low-income, inner-city residents. Shaw is on the frontier between rising affluence and stubborn poverty. It is experiencing gentrification and racial change. And even the black population is no longer just African Americans. A cluster of Ethiopian restaurants, for example, bears witness to immigration from Africa. New immigrants are reshaping the traditional black-white divide.

An area that was disengaged from mainstream Megalopolis from the 1960s to the 1990s is now caught up in a process of incorporation. It is becoming more racially mixed, more economically connected to the rest of the metropolitan economy. Zones of abandonment are being reclaimed. There are tensions in this process. Paul Schwartzman (2006) writes of a bittersweet renaissance as some of the original black residents see their property values increase but worry about the changing character of the neighborhood; some black churches rail against the more open examples of gay culture; others complain about the designation of part of U Street as Little Ethiopia as disrespectful of the long African American heritage in the area. Spiking property prices and rents have raised issues of housing affordability for long-term residents and their families. Shaw is a liminal zone between two very segregated and different parts of the city. Its fluidity embodies the liquid nature of Megalopolis. A consideration of the creation of a more racially mixed, more diverse community with all the attendant tensions, opportunities, and dangers is a good place to conclude a discussion of Megalopolis at the beginning of the 21st century.

FINAL THOUGHTS

Before concluding let me draw a wider arc. Megalopolis is one of the most important urban regions in the United States and indeed in the world. Its internal coherence has deepened as lengthening journeys to work, widening regional job markets, and dispersing housing markets effectively link the separate metros into overlapping fields of influence and interconnecting flows of people and goods. Megalopolis is a region in itself. Whether it will become a region *for* itself, with a conscious sense of shared identity—a distinction first discussed in Chapter 2—is more debatable. Local identities, allegiance, and political realities all work to balkanize Megalopolis. And yet there is the increasing sense that such problems as transport congestion, affordable housing, pollution, waste management, and economic competitiveness are not only similar around the region, they are shared problems whose solutions require wider regional systems of cooperation. Take the case of rail transport. Table 12-1 compares the cost and time of train journeys between selected cities in Megalopolis with cities in other megalopolitan regions. Notice how for journeys of similar distance, either the cost or the time and in some cases both are greater in Megalopolis than in the other pairs of cities. These extra costs, and others like them, feed into the global economic competitiveness of the region. In a globalized economy, inefficiencies are severely punished.

The balkanization of the region is economically inefficient. Example one: the poverty of central city schools creates low educational attainment, which results in poorly skilled labor, yet in a global economy, developed city regions need highly skilled labor. Example two: municipalities want jobs and commercial developments but often limit housing developments. The former generate tax revenue, the latter generate demands on municipal budgets. Municipalities thus try to attract jobs and steer away housing. The result is sprawl, as people have to drive to find the housing they can afford. The national ranking of counties and cities with "extreme commutes,"

Table 12-1. Comparison of Train Journeys, 2006

Connecting cities	Distance	Time	Cost
Baltimore to New York	190 miles	161 mins.	$80
Rome to Florence	197 miles	100 mins.	$36
Philadelphia to Boston	268 miles	360 mins.	$91
Tokyo to Kyoto	229 miles	150 mins.	$113
Washington to Boston	440 miles	480 mins.	$101
Florence to Nice	459 miles	520 mins.	$48

Source: Based on Fradkin (2006).

defined as traveling 90 minutes or more each working day, is led by Mega-lopolitan counties and cities (Table 12-2). Again, extra costs impinge on economic competitiveness as well as put strains on households having to journey farther to work.

I do not propose a Megalopolitan government, since this is not politi-cally feasible. Affluent suburban municipalities do not want to be annexed by cash-starved central cities. Rather, I am suggesting a more explicit con-sideration of wider, regional systems of cooperation and the beginnings of a political awareness of the shared fate of the multiple municipalities and counties that constitute this region. Megalopolis is an economic unit that lacks political representation or systems of governance, and if this contin-ues without more regional cooperation, the failing will affect the economic competitiveness of the region in the national and global economy.

Megalopolis plays a significant role in the economic and political life of the nation. It is the single largest megalopolitan region in the country, and it continues to be a center for population, economic growth, and vitality; it is responsible for one-fifth of the nation's economic activity. Although it has lost much of its edge as a manufacturing center, it retains dominance in advanced producer services as well as professional, scientific, and technical services. It is also globally significant as a center for economic and political

Table 12-2. Extreme Commuting Times in Cities and Counties in Megalopolis, 2003

City	Percentage extreme commuters	National rank
Baltimore	5.6	1
New York	5.6	1
Newark, NJ	5.2	2
Philadelphia	2.9	5
Washington	2.2	7
County		
Richmond, NY	11.8	1
Orange, NY	10.0	2
Queens, NY	7.1	3
Bronx, NY	6.9	4
Nassau, NY	6.6	6
Kings, NY	5.0	7
Prince William, VA	4.5	9
Prince George's, MD	3.8	10
Montgomery, MD	2.2	11

Note: "Extreme commuter" is defined as a worker over 16 years who travels 90 minutes or more to and from the workplace.
Source: U.S. Census, American Community Survey, http://www.census.gov/acs/www/index.html (accessed October 2, 2006).

globalization, one of the principal organizing hubs of a global economy. The region maintains its national preeminence and its global dominance. But if it continues as a region in itself rather than for itself, the internal inefficiencies will ultimately undermine its centrality to both the nation and the world.

Finally, let us return to the question posed in the first chapter. Geddes saw megalopolis, the idea, as the final stage in an inexorable decline. Gottmann, in contrast, saw Megalopolis, the place, as a harbinger of a new way of life. Which is correct, the gloomy formulation of Geddes or the sunnier claim of Gottmann? There are no simple answers to starkly framed questions. However, the reality favors Gottmann rather than Geddes. Megalopolis poses problems, major problems no doubt, but it is the forward edge of history. The future lies in the fate of such giant city regions as Megalopolis.

REFERENCES

Alexander, M.L. 1967. *The Northeastern United States*. Princeton: Nostrand.

Anonymous. 2003. California Sprawl; Endless Los Angelization Is Winning Approval. *San Diego Union Tribune*, June 8, G2.

Baigent, E. 2004. Patrick Geddes, Lewis Mumford and Jean Gottmann: Divisions over "Megalopolis." *Progress in Human Geography* 28: 687–700.

Bauman, Z. 1992. *Intimations of Postmodernity*. London: Routledge.

———. 2005. *Liquid Life*. Cambridge: Polity.

Benton-Short, L., M.D. Price, and S. Friedman. 2005. Globalization from Below: The Ranking of Global Immigrant Cities. *International Journal of Urban and Regional Research* 29: 945–59.

Bernstein, J., E. McNichol, and K. Lyons. 2006. *Pulling Apart: A State by State Analysis of Income Trends*. Washington, DC: Economic Policy Institute and Center on Budget and Policy Priorities.

Berube, A., and T. Tiffany. 2005. The Shape of the Curve: Household Income Distributions in U.S. Cities, 1979–99. In A. Berube, B. Katz, and R. Lang (eds.), *Redefining Urban and Suburban America: Evidence from Census 2000*, vol. 2. Washington, DC: Brookings Institution Press, 195-243.

Bogue, D. 1951. *State Economic Areas*. Washington, DC: U.S. Government Printing Office.

Borchert, J.R. 1992. *Megalopolis: Washington D.C. to Boston*. New Brunswick, NJ: Rutgers University Press.

Breugmann, R. 2005. *Sprawl: A Compact History*. Chicago: University of Chicago Press.

Brueckner, J.K., and Y. Zenou. 2003. Space and Unemployment: The Labor-Market Effects of Spatial Mismatch. *Journal of Labor Economics* 21: 242–62.

Carbonell, A., and R. Yaro. 2005. American Spatial Development and the New Megalopolis. *Landlines* April: 1–4.

Cooper, D.R., and P.S. Schindler. 2003. *Business Research Methods*, 8th ed. New York: McGraw-Hill Higher Education.

Dear, M. (ed.). 2001. *From Chicago to LA: Making Sense of Urban Theory*. New York: Russell Sage.

De Certeau, M. 1984. *The Practice of Everyday Life*. Berkeley: University of California Press.

Downey, K. 2005. Suburbs by the Sea. *The Washington Post*, July 9, F1, F13.

Fasenfest, D., J. Booza, and K. Metzger. 2004. *Living Together: A New Look at Racial and Ethnic Integration in Metropolitan Neighborhoods, 1990–2000*. Washington, DC: Brookings Institution Press.

Florida, R. 2006. A Creative Crossroads. *The Washington Post*, May 7, B3.

Foner, N. (ed.). 2001. *New Immigrants in New York*. New York: Columbia University Press.

Foner, N. 2005. *In a New Land: A Comparative View of Immigration*. New York: New York University Press.

Fradkin, A. 2006. Megalopolitan Power in America. Unpublished paper. Department of Public Policy. University of Maryland Baltimore County.

Friedman, T.L. 2005. *The World Is Flat*. New York: Farrar, Strauss and Giroux.

Galster, G., R. Hanson, M. Ratcliffe, H. Wolman, S. Coleman, and J. Freihage. 2001. Wrestling Sprawl to the Ground: Defining and Measuring an Elusive Concept. *Housing Policy Debate* 12: 681–717.

Gans, H. 1962. *The Urban Villagers*. New York: Free Press.

Garreau, J. 1991. *Edge Cities: Life on the New Frontier*. New York: Doubleday.

Gottmann, J. 1957. Megalopolis or the Urbanization of the Northeastern Seaboard. *Economic Geography* 33: 189–200.

———. 1961. *Megalopolis*. New York: Twentieth Century Fund.

————. 1987. *Megalopolis Revisited*. College Park, MD: University of Maryland Institute for Urban Studies.

Gottmann, J., and R.A. Harper. 1990. *Since Megalopolis: The Urban Writings of Jean Gottmann*. Baltimore and London: Johns Hopkins University Press.

Hall, P. 1973. *The Containment of Urban England*. London: Allen and Unwin.

Hanlon, B., and T. Vicino. 2005. *The State of the Inner Suburbs: An Examination of Suburban Baltimore, 1980 to 2000*. University of Maryland Baltimore County: Center for Urban Environmental Research and Education.

Hanlon, B., T. Vicino, and J.R. Short. 2006. The New Metropolitan Reality: Rethinking the Traditional Model. *Urban Studies* 43: 2129–43.

Harris, C. 1982. The Urban and Industrial Transformation of Japan. *Geographical Review* 72: 50–89.

Hudnut III, W.H. 2003. *Halfway to Everywhere: A Portrait of America's First Tier Suburbs*. Washington, DC: Urban Land Institute.

Jargowsky, P.A. 2003. Stunning Progress, Hidden Problems: The Dramatic Decline of Concentrated Poverty in the 1990s. *Living Cities Census Series*. Metropolitan Policy Program. Washington, DC: Brookings Institution Press.

Jargowsky, P.A., and R. Yang. 2006. The "Underclass" Revisited: A Social Problem in Decline. *Journal of Urban Affairs* 28: 55–70.

Judd, D. R., and T. Swanstrom. 2006. *City Politics: The Political Economy of Urban America*. New York: Pearson Longman.

Kain, J. 1993. The Spatial Mismatch Hypothesis: Three Decades Later. *Housing Policy Debate* 3: 371–460.

Kingsley, T., and K. Pettit. 2006. America's Inner City Neighborhoods; What Has Happened since 2000? Paper presented to the Urban Affairs Annual Conference, Montreal, April 20.

Kirp, D.L., J.P. Dwyer, and L.A. Rosenthal. 1995. *Our Town: Race, Housing and the Soul of Suburbia*. New Brunswick, NJ: Rutgers University Press.

Kozol, J. 1991. *Savage Inequalities*. New York: Crown.

————. 2000. *Ordinary Resurrections: Children in the Year of Hope*. New York: Crown.

————. 2005. *Shame of the Nation: The Restoration of Apartheid Schooling in America*. New York: Crown.

Kunkle, F. 2006. Frederick Growth Squeezes Affordable Housing. *The Washington Post*, January 29, C4.

Kunstler, J.H. 1993. *The Geography of Nowhere*. New York: Touchstone.

Lake, R. 2003. *Gottmann Forty Years On*. Unpublished paper based on panel discussion at Association of American Geographers Mid States Geography Conference, Albany, October.

Lang, R.E. 2003a. *Edgeless Cities: Exploring the Elusive Metropolis*. Washington, DC: Brookings Institution Press.

———. 2003b. Open Bounded Places: Does the American West's Arid Landscape Yield Dense Metropolitan Growth? *Housing Policy Debate* 13: 755–78.

Lang, R.E., and Dhavale, D. 2005a. Beyond Megalopolis: Exploring America's New "Megapolitan" Geography. Metropolitan Institute of Virginia Tech. Census Report 05: 01.

———. 2005b. The 2005 Governor's Race. Metropolitan Institute of Virginia Tech. Election Brief.

Lang, R.E., T. Sanchez, and J. LeFurgy. 2006. *Beyond Edgeless Cities: Office Geography in the New Metropolis*. Metropolitan Institute of Virginia Tech.

Lewis, R. 2005. Smart Growth in Maryland: Fitting More Groceries in the Same Bag. *The Washington Post*, November 12, F5.

Lipton, E. 2001. City Trash Follows a Long and Winding Road. *The New York Times*, March 24, B1, B5.

Lucy, W.H., and D.L. Phillips. 2000. *Confronting Suburban Decline: Strategic Planning for Metropolitan Renewal*. Washington, DC: Island Press.

MacGillis, A. 2006. Ties to Far-Flung Homes Drive Commuters to Great Lengths. *The Washington Post*, April 25, A1, A12.

McCrummen, S. 2006. On Edge of Va. Sprawl, Labels Crumble, New Lives Thrive, *The Washington Post*, March 27, A1, A9.

Metropolitan Washington Council of Governments and the National Park Service. 2004. *Increase in Developed Land Map within the Metropolitan Washington Region, 1986–2000*. Washington, DC: Metropolitan Washington Council of Governments.

Morrill, R. 2006. Classic Map Revisited: The Growth of Megalopolis. *The Professional Geographer* 58: 155–60.

Moynihan, D.P. 1969. Toward a National Urban Policy. *Public Interest* 17: 3–20.

Mumford, L. 1961. *The City in History*. New York: Harcourt Brace.

Norris, D.F. 2001. Prospects for Regional Governance under the New Regionalism: Economic Imperatives versus Political Impediments. *Journal of Urban Affairs* 23: 557–71.

Orfield, M. 2002. *American Metropolitics: The New Suburban Reality*. Washington, DC: Brookings Institution Press.

Orser, W. E. 1994. *Blockbusting in Baltimore: The Edmondson Village Story.* Lexington: University Press of Kentucky.

Osborn, F.J., and A. Whittick. 1963. *The New Towns: The Answer to Megalopolis.* London: McGraw-Hill.

Paley, A.R. 2005. Region's Fringes Draw a "New White Flight." *The Washington Post,* May 11, A1, A9.

Pell, C. 1966. *Megalopolis Unbound: The Supercity and the Transportation of Tomorrow.* New York: Praeger.

Puentes, R., and D. Warren. 2006. *One-Fifth of America: A Comprehensive Guide to America's First Suburbs.* Washington, DC: Brookings Institution Press.

Putnam, R. 2000. *Bowling Alone: The Collapse and Revival of American Community.* New York: Simon and Schuster.

Putnam, S.H. 1975. *An Empirical Model of Regional Growth: With an Application to the Northeast Megalopolis.* Philadelphia: Regional Science Institute.

Rusk, D. 1999. *Inside Game Outside Game.* Washington, DC: Brookings Institution Press.

———. 2003. *Cities without Suburbs: A Census 2000 Update.* Washington, DC: Woodrow Wilson Center Press.

Savitch, H.V., and R.K. Vogel. 2004. Suburbs without a City: Power and City-County Consolidation. *Urban Affairs Review* 39: 758–90.

Schwartz, J. 2003. Imagining Central Texas, 20–40 Years Down the Road. *Austin American Statesman,* October 5, A1.

Schwartzman, P. 2006. A Bittersweet Renaissance. *The Washington Post,* February 23, A1, A8, A9.

Scott, A.J. (ed). 2001. *Global City Regions.* Oxford: Oxford University Press.

Scott, A.J., and E.W. Soja (eds.). 1996. *The City: Los Angeles and Urban Theory at the End of the Twentieth Century.* Berkeley: University of California Press.

Shevky, E., and Q. Bell. 1955. *Social Area Analysis: Theory and Illustrative Application and Computational Procedure.* Stanford, CA: Stanford University Press.

Short, J.R. 1978. Residential Mobility in the Private Housing Market of Bristol. *Transactions of the Institute of British Geographers, New Series* 4: 533–47.

———. 2004. *Global Metropolitan.* London and New York: Routledge.

———. 2006. *Urban Theory: A Critical Assessment.* London: Palgrave Macmillan.

———. 2006. *Alabaster Cities: Urban U.S. Since 1950.* Syracuse, NY: Syracuse University Press.

Short, J.R., L.M. Benton, W.B. Luce, and J. Walton. 1993. Reconstructing the Image of an Industrial City. *Annals of Association of American Geographers* 83: 207–24.

Short, J.R., S. Fleming, and S. Witt. 1986. *Housebuilding, Planning and Community Action*. London: Routledge and Kegan Paul.

Simmons, P. 2005. Rising Affordability Problems among Homeowners. *Fannie Mae Foundation* Census Note 13.

Singer, A. 2005. The Rise of New Immigrant Gateways: Historical Flows, Recent Settlement Trends. In A. Berube, B. Katz, and R.E. Lang (eds.), *Redefining Urban and Suburban America: Evidence from Census 2000*, vol. 2. Washington, DC: Brookings Institution Press, 41–86.

Singer, M. 2003. The Haves and the Haves. *The New Yorker*, August 11, 56–61.

Spivack, M.S. 2005. A Rising Tempest Confronts Howard's Growth. *The Washington Post*, July 10, C1, C5.

Stevens, D., R. Clinch, and J. Staveley. 2001. *Job Availability for Recipients of Temporary Cash Assistance*. Baltimore: Jacob France Institute, University of Baltimore.

Swanstrom, T., C. Casey, R. Flack, and P. Dreier. 2004. Pulling Apart: Economic Segregation among Suburbs and Central Cities in Major Metropolitan Areas. Washington, DC: Brookings Institution Press.

Taeuber, I., and C. Taeuber. 1964. The Great Concentration: SMSA's from Boston to Washington. *Population Index* 30: 3–29.

Taylor, P.J. 2004. *Global City Network*. London: Routledge.

Taylor, P.J., and R. Aranya. 2006. A Global 'Urban Roller Coaster'? Connectivity Changes in the World City Network, 2000–04. GAWC Research Bulletin 192. http://www.lboro.ac.uk/gawc/rb/rb192.html (accessed May 8, 2006).

Taylor, P.J., and R. Lang. 2005. *U.S. Cities in the 'World City Network'*. Washington, DC: The Brookings Institution Survey Series.

Taylor, P.J., B. Derudder, and F. Witlox. 2006. Comparing Airline Passenger Destinations with Global Service Connectivities: A Worldwide Empirical Study of 214 Cities. GAWC Research Bulletin 196. http://www.lboro.ac.uk/gawc/rb/rb196.html (accessed May 8, 2006).

Townsend, A. 2001. The Internet and the Rise of the New Network Cities, 1969–2000. *Environment and Planning B; Planning and Design* 28: 39–58.

U.S. Department of Housing and Urban Development. 2005. *The Sustainability of Homeownership*. www.huduser.org/publications/affhsg/homeownsustainability.html (accessed June 10, 2006).

Vickerman, M. 2001. "Tweaking a Monolith": The West Indian Encounter with "Blackness." In N. Foner (ed.), *New Immigrants in New York*. New York: Columbia University Press.

Volstad, J.H., N.E. Roth, G. Mercurio, M.T. Southerland, and D.E. Strebel. 2003. Using Environmental Stressor Information to Predict the Ecological Status of

Maryland Non-Tidal Streams as Measured by Biological Indicators. *Environmental Monitoring and Assessment* 84: 219–42.

Wade, M. (ed.). 1969. *The International Megalopolis*. Toronto: University of Toronto Press.

Waldinger, R. (ed.). 2001. *Strangers at the Gates: New Immigrants in Urban America*. Berkeley: University of California Press.

Weller, R.H. 1967. An Empirical Examination of Megalopolitan Structure. *Demography* 4: 734–43.

Williamson, E. 2004. Region's Green Space Going Fast. *The Washington Post*, May 22, B1, B5.

Wilson, W.J. 1996. *When Work Disappears: The World of the New Urban Poor*. New York: Knopf.

Wong, D.W.S. 2003. Spatial Decomposition of Segregation Indices. *Geographical Analysis* 35: 179–95.

Wong, D.W.S. 2004. The Modifiable Areal Unit Problem (MAUP). In D. Janelle, B. Warf, and K. Hansen (eds.), *WorldMinds: Geographical Perspectives on 100 Problems*. Dordrecht: Kluwer, 571–75.

INDEX

Note: Figures and tables are indicated with a lower case "f" and "t", respectively.

ABOUT THE AUTHOR

John Rennie Short is professor of public policy at the University of Maryland, Baltimore County. His research has focused on the measurement of globalization in cities and the assessment of urban environmental policies. He has published numerous academic papers and books, including *Alabaster Cities*, *Urban Theory*, *Globalization and the City*, and *Global Metropolitan*.

DATE		
	WITHDRAWN	